D1078683   T

HOUSTON
& THE TEXAS GULF COAST

ANDY RHODES

Contents

Houston and East Texas..................7

Planning Your Time...............10

Information and Services.........10

Getting There and Around........11

Houston.......................12

Sights............................13
- 🄲 NASA Space Center...............13
- 🄲 Contemporary Arts Museum of Houston..............17
- Museum of Natural Science.........17
- Houston Museum of Fine Arts.......17
- 🄲 The Orange Show................18
- San Jacinto Battleground-Battleship *Texas* State Historic Sites.........18
- The Health Museum.................19
- Houston Zoo......................19
- Children's Museum of Houston......20
- The Menil Collection................21
- 🄲 The Kemah Boardwalk............21
- The Water Wall....................21
- Houston Arboretum and Nature Center....................22
- Downtown Aquarium...............22
- Bayou Bend Collection..............22
- George Ranch Historical Park.......23
- Smaller Museums..................23

Entertainment and Events.......24
- Performing Arts...................24
- Live Music.......................25
- Bars and Clubs...................26
- Events............................28

Shopping........................28
- Downtown.......................28
- Uptown..........................29
- Rice Village-Kirby District...........29
- Southwest Houston................29
- Katy Outlet Stores.................30

Sports and Recreation...........30
- Professional Sports...............30
- Parks............................31
- Hiking and Biking..................31
- Golf.............................32

Accommodations.................32

Food.............................35

Information and Services.........40

Getting There and Around.......40

Beaumont and Vicinity..........40
- 🄲 Spindletop-Gladys City Boomtown Museum..............41
- McFaddin-Ward House.............41
- Texas Energy Museum.............42
- Fire Museum of Texas.............42
- Babe Didrickson Zaharias Museum...42
- Accommodations..................43
- Food............................43
- Information and Services..........44
- Port Arthur......................44
- Orange..........................46

Piney Woods..................47

🄲 Big Thicket National Preserve..47

National Forests.................49
- Angelina National Forest...........49
- Davy Crockett National Forest......50
- Sabine National Forest............51
- Sam Houston National Forest.......52

Alabama-Coushatta Indian Reservation............53

Lufkin..........................53
- Texas Forestry Museum............54
- Museum of East Texas.............54
- The History Center................54
- Accommodations..................55

Food 55
Information and Services 56

Nacogdoches and Vicinity 56
Old Stone Fort Museum 56
Sterne-Hoya House 56
Stephen F. Austin
    Experimental Forest 56
◖ Texas State Railroad 57
Caddo Mounds State Historic Site 58
Accommodations 58
Food 59
Information and Services 59

Tyler 59
Tyler Municipal Rose
    Garden and Museum 60
Plantation Museums 61
Caldwell Zoo .62
Tyler Museum of Art 62
Accommodations 62
Food 63
Information and Services 63

Jefferson 63
Historic Buildings 64
The Atalanta Railroad Car 65
Scarlett O'Hardy's Gone With
    the Wind Museum 65
Lake o' the Pines 65
◖ Caddo Lake 66
Accommodations 66
Food 67
Information and Services 67

The Gulf Coast 68

Planning Your Time 70

Information and Services 71

Getting There and Around 72

Galveston .72

Sights 73
◖ The Strand .73
Museums 73
◖ The *Elissa* .77

Moody Gardens 77

Shopping 79
The Strand 79

Accommodations 79

Food 81

Recreation 84
Beaches 84

Information and Services 84

Getting There and Around 84

Brazosport Area 84
Sights and Recreation 85
Beaches 85
Brazoria National Wildlife Refuge 85
San Bernard National Wildlife Refuge .86
Fishing 86
Accommodations 86
Food 87
Information and Services 87

**Corpus Christi
    and Vicinity** 88

Sights 88
◖ Texas State Aquarium 88
◖ USS *Lexington* Museum 88
Corpus Christi Museum of
    Science and History 90
Heritage Park .90
Asian Cultures Museum 90
Selena Museum 91
Art Museum of South Texas 91
Corpus Christi Botanical Gardens
    and Nature Center 92

Recreation 92
Beaches 92
◖ Padre Island National Seashore 92
Fishing 93
Windsurfing 94
Horseback Riding 94

Entertainment 94
Bars and Clubs 94

Shopping 95

Accommodations 95

Food 97

Information and Services 99

Getting There and Around 99

Port Aransas 100
Marine Science Institute 100
San Jose Island 100
Fishing 100
Swimming 101
Accommodations 101
Food 102
Information and Services 103

Kingsville 103
◖ King Ranch .103
1904 Train Depot and Museum 104
Kenedy Ranch Museum
    of South Texas 106
John E. Conner Museum 106
Accommodations 107
Food 107
Information and Services 108

South Padre Island 108

Sights 108
Sea Turtle, Inc. 109
Dolphin Research and
    Sea Life Nature Center 109
◖ Port Isabel Lighthouse 109
Pan American Coastal
    Studies Laboratory 110
Schlitterbahn Beach Waterpark 110

Recreation 110
Swimming 110
Fishing 110
Dolphin Viewing 111
Snorkeling and Scuba Diving 111

Accommodations 112

Food 113

Information and Services 115

Getting There and Around 115

HOUSTON
& THE TEXAS GULF COAST

HOUSTON AND EAST TEXAS

Like the mountains more than 800 miles to the west, the pine forests of East Texas are another natural wonder not typically associated with the Lone Star State. Not surprisingly, the cultural gap between the two regions is as wide as their distance apart.

East Texas has a distinct Southern bayou influence, reflected in the region's food, heritage, and even the accent. Locals are much more likely to regale visitors with long stories in their laiiid-baaack, draaaawn-out speaking style than their twangy tight-lipped West Texan counterparts. Standing apart from this rural Southern character is the megapolis of Houston, the fourth-largest city in the country and home to NASA, oil-related industries, and some of the preeminent museums (and humidity) in the country.

East Texas has long been the gateway to the Lone Star State because its earliest inhabitants—Native Americans, European explorers, Anglo settlers, and African-Americans—arrived primarily from Eastern locales. One of the first things they encountered was the dense acreage now known as the Piney Woods, which includes several national forests and the Big Thicket Preserve.

One of the first groups to inhabit the area was the Caddo Indians, an advanced tribe with sophisticated trade networks throughout the region. The Caddos are credited with inspiring the name Texas, since they welcomed the Spanish explorers by referring to them as *tejas,* meaning friends or allies. By the 1700s, Spain attempted to fortify its presence in the area by establishing a series of missions to protect their

HIGHLIGHTS

❰ NASA Space Center: For a true otherworldly experience, shoot over to NASA, Houston's preeminent tourist attraction. Don't miss the awe-inspiring Mission Control building (page 13).

❰ Contemporary Arts Museum of Houston: One of the country's most respected modern art facilities, the Contemporary Arts Museum offers a compelling collection of paintings, sculpture, and objets d'art in a stunning stainless-steel building (page 17).

❰ The Orange Show: Postman-turned-artist Jeff McKissack glorified "the perfect food" by devoting thousands of square feet to orange-related folk art, including sculptures, masonry, and bizarre buildings (page 18).

❰ The Kemah Boardwalk: Located southwest of Houston on Galveston Bay, the boardwalk is pretty touristy but offers nostalgic fun with amusement park rides, a massive aquarium, and a train along with restaurants, shops, and fountains at the water's edge (page 21).

❰ Spindletop-Gladys City Boomtown Museum: The 1901 oil gush heard 'round the country erupted at this site chronicling Beaumont's boomtown days (page 41).

❰ Big Thicket National Preserve: This swath of East Texas Piney Woods contains a gaggle of species from the Gulf Coast, Central Plains, and Southeastern forests coexisting with critters from the deserts, bayous, woods, and swamps (page 47).

❰ Texas State Railroad: Experience the old-time feel of riding the rails on this rickety yet enchanting locomotive, which chugs, clanks, and charms its way through the East Texas Piney Woods (page 57).

❰ Caddo Lake: Though it's way up in the northeast corner of the state, Caddo Lake, the only natural lake in Texas, is worth a visit for its scenic backdrop of wispy Spanish moss and outstretched cypress trees while hiking, swimming, fishing, or boating (page 66).

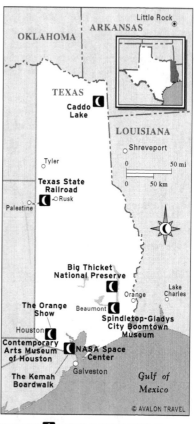

LOOK FOR ❰ TO FIND RECOMMENDED SIGHTS, ACTIVITIES, DINING, AND LODGING.

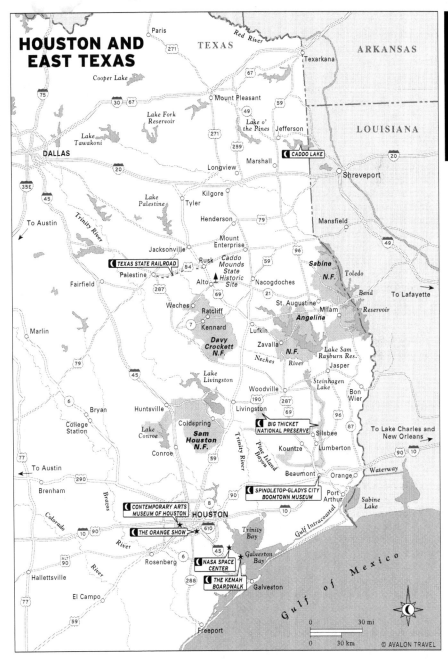

HOUSTON AND EAST TEXAS

© AVALON TRAVEL

political interests (especially against meddle-some France) and to "civilize" the native population by converting them to Catholicism. Neither of these ventures was very successful, so the land remained relatively unoccupied until Anglo homesteaders began arriving in large numbers in the early 1800s. In the southern portion of this region just west of modern-day Houston, a group of settlers known as the Old Three Hundred established Stephen F. Austin's initial colony. After the fall of the Alamo in March 1836, droves of frightened frontier families fled to East Texas in an event known as the Runaway Scrape.

By the late 1800s, the region became associated with industry. Railroad expansion and European immigration brought an increased population and entrepreneurs, and the new railroad lines provided access to the Piney Woods's interiors, allowing the lumber industry to flourish. A few decades later, Texas's identity was forever changed when the 100-foot-high oil spout known as the Lucas Gusher blew in (the industry term for erupting) near Beaumont. As soon as word spread about the gusher's subterranean Spindletop oil field, tens of thousands of people flocked to the area to make (or lose) their fortunes. The colorfully named roughnecks and wildcatters worked the fields, while the entrepreneurial-minded investors made the money.

In 1901, the first year of the boom, three major oil companies—Gulf, Humble (later Exxon), and Texas (later Texaco)—formed in Beaumont, and by the following year there were 500 corporations in town. The impact of Spindletop and other oil fields discovered near Tyler is immeasurable, as it brought billions of dollars to Texas through oil company profits and related industry endeavors. Houston perhaps benefited the most, since the oil business ultimately shifted most of its headquarters and shipping operations to the city, which grew at phenomenal rates throughout the mid-1900s.

As a result of this intriguing history, East Texas has a remarkable number of heritage tourism and cultural destinations for visitors to explore. From Caddoan Indian burial mounds to historic logging towns to Southern plantation homes, oil boomtowns, and five national forests, this widespread region is an ideal place to experience the enormous legacy of the Lone Star State.

PLANNING YOUR TIME

Houston is often considered more of a business obligation than a tourist destination, which is unfortunate, since many of the city's museums and cultural attractions are first-rate. Those who make the effort to visit, be it for personal or professional reasons, will discover several days' worth of intriguing activities. NASA is a must, and the downtown museum district and restaurants will keep visitors occupied for at least two if not three days. History buffs should devote half a day to the state park 20 miles east of town containing the impressive San Jacinto Monument and Battleship *Texas.*

The remaining vast expanse of East Texas is worth spending three or four days exploring, depending on the amount of time and energy available for seeking adventure among the Piney Woods and Deep South surroundings. Beaumont is a fun day trip from Houston (less than two hours away), especially for those who want to learn everything they ever wanted to know about Texas's oil legacy. Naturalists should set aside a day or two to explore the Big Thicket National Preserve and other nearby national forests, and visitors interested in old-fashioned Southern culture are encouraged to spend a few days in the northern portion of the Piney Woods, where the cities of Tyler, Lufkin, and Jefferson exude Texas's true heritage.

INFORMATION AND SERVICES

Since Houston isn't a big-time vacation destination, it doesn't have an abundance of travelers' bureaus offering maps and brochures. In fact, it only has one. Fortunately, the **Greater Houston Convention and Visitors Bureau** (901 Bagby St., Suite 100, 713/437-5200, www.visithoustontexas.com, daily 9 A.M.–4 P.M.) can handle just about everything. The CVB's impressive offices at City Hall (Bagby Street location) are chock-full of literature and knowledgeable staff members, and the bureau offers similar services at satellite offices at the Bay Area Houston Visitors Center (on Hwy. 45 about 15 miles southeast of town, 281/338-0333) and a kiosk at Katy Mills Mall (on I-10 about 15 miles west of town).

Tours of Houston and the surrounding area are also available. Contact **HoustonTours. net** (888/838-5894, www.houstontours.net) to choose from activity types or location. The site also offers a selection of "most popular tours," including motorcycle rentals and helicopter rides in the area. Another company, **Houston Tours, Inc.** (8915 Bellaire Blvd., 713/988-5900, www.houstontours.com, daily 8 A.M.–8 P.M.) features traditional bus tours of downtown, outlying neighborhoods, and treks to Galveston.

For something more educational (and quirky), consider taking part in one of the Orange Show Foundation's **Eyeopener Tours** (713/926-6368, www.orangeshow.org/eyeopener-tours, typically held the second weekend of the month). Inspired by "places that made you stop, look and look again," Eyeopener Tours are dedicated to itineraries involving compelling food, stories, and sightings in the Houston area and beyond. Tours typically involve a fancy bus with snacks and drinks (averaging around $65 for the entire package) en route to the interesting objet d'folk art, architectural wonders (or disasters), and enigmatic ethnic enclaves of the city.

For those venturing beyond Bayou City, the **Texas Forest Trail Region** (headquarters 202 E. Pilar St. #214, Nacogdoches, 936/560-3699, www.texasforesttrail.com) is an ideal place to prepare for a Piney Woods adventure. Check out the website or drop by the main office to get help with determining an East Texas itinerary. For detailed information about travel options in the region's smaller communities, contact the local convention and visitors bureau or chamber of commerce, listed at the end of the corresponding sections in this chapter.

If you're entering East Texas by vehicle from Louisiana, look for the Texas Department of Transportation's **Travel Information Center** at two spots on the state border. The largest facility is in Orange (1708 E. I-10, 409/883-9416) on I-10 en route from New Orleans. The other is in Waskom (1255 N. I-20 E., 903/687-2547) on I-20 from Shreveport. Visit www.dot.state.tx.us for road-related travel information, or check out www.tx.roadconnect.net to find out about the nearest rest area or travel center with free Wi-Fi access.

The best source for news and information in Houston and southeast Texas is the **Houston Chronicle** (www.chron.com), containing thorough coverage of city and state happenings, as well as detailed listings of restaurants and entertainment venues. For specific information about local politics, touring shows, and movie listings, pick up a free copy of the **Houston Press** (www.houstonpress.com) at bars, coffee shops, and bus stations across town.

GETTING THERE AND AROUND

Houston is so big, it has two airports. The rest of the cities in East Texas aren't that big, but several have small regional airports to save travelers the long drives through forests and marshy grasslands.

The major air hub in this part of the country is **George Bush Intercontinental Airport** (2800 N. Terminal Rd., 281/230-3100, www.fly2houston.com), located just north of Houston. This is one of Continental Airlines's major hubs, and since it offers non-stop service to and from more than 170 cities around the world, it's typically hustling and bustling at all hours of the day and night. The city's old airfield, **William P. Hobby Airport** (7800 Airport Blvd., 713/640-3000, www.fly2houston.com) is now the center of activity for Southwest Airlines and hosts flights from several other major carriers. Located 10 miles southeast of downtown, Hobby is more accessible than Bush, but it's showing its age. That's often forgivable by travelers who prefer the facilitated accessibility and cheaper cab fares (nearly $20 less than the trek from Bush to downtown Houston).

SuperShuttle (281/230-7275, www.supershuttle.com) offers shuttle service to and from area hotels and Bush Intercontinental and Hobby Airports. Look for the company's ticket counters in the lower level baggage claim areas of Bush and Hobby. Many downtown-area hotels offer free shuttle service to and from Bush Intercontinental Airport, but check first to make sure they're running.

Another option is a cab. Ground transportation employees outside each terminal of Bush Intercontinental Airport and near the lower level baggage claim area (Curbzone 1) of Hobby Airport will half-heartedly hail travelers a taxi. All destinations within Houston's city limits to/from Bush Intercontinental are charged a flat zone rate or the meter rate, whichever is less. For more information on zone rates, check out the Ground Transportation section at www.fly2houston.com. To arrange for cab pick-up service from within the city, contact one of the following local companies: **Liberty Cab Company** (281/540-8294), **Square Deal Cab Co.** (713/444-4444), **Lonestar Cab** (713/794-0000), and **United Cab Co.** (713/699-0000).

Many travelers prefer to rent a car, and the powers that be at Bush Intercontinental have attempted to make things easier by establishing the **Consolidated Rental Car Facility** (281/230-3000, www.iahrac.com). All the major rental car companies are accessible from this shared location about five minutes away from the terminals. The rental companies share a shuttle system, designated by the white and maroon buses marked "Rental Car Shuttle" located outside the terminal.

Houston is large enough to make accessibility by bus and train a viable option (thanks to the frequency in arrivals and departures). Those interested in traveling by bus can contact **Houston Greyhound** (2121 Main St., 713/759-6565 or 800/231-2222, www.greyhound.com). Passenger trains arrive in town via **Amtrak's Sunset Limited** line, which runs cross-country between Orlando and Los Angeles. Look for arrivals and departures at the Houston Amtrak station (902 Washington Ave., 713/224-1577 or 800/872-7245, www.amtrak.com).

Houston has a decent public transportation system, but it can be confusing for out-of-towners who haven't yet developed a strong sense of direction. Regardless, a little homework can be helpful in strategizing plans via the Metro, aka the **Metropolitan Transit Authority of Harris County** (713/635-4000, www.ridemetro.org), which offers local and commuter bus service. Tickets are available in vending machines located at each station. Metro's red line services 16 stations near downtown's busiest commercial and recreational sites.

Houston

A city as big as Houston (metro population 2,144,491) deserves to be named after a larger-than-life figure: Sam Houston, president of the Republic of Texas who, as general of the Texas army, led the fight for independence from Mexico. Everything about Houston is huge—with more than five million people in the area, it's the largest city in Texas and fourth largest in the country. The Bayou City is notorious for its lack of zoning ordinances and its high humidity, resulting in unmitigated sprawl and unbearably hot summers. But it's not without its charm—Houston has world-class cultural and medical facilities, and its immense international population contributes to a truly cosmopolitan setting with world-renowned corporations, services, and restaurants.

The city even started out with grand ambitions. In the late 1830s, New York City brothers and entrepreneurs Augustus and John Allen claimed that the town would become the "great interior commercial emporium of Texas," with ships from New York and New Orleans sailing up Buffalo Bayou to its door. For most of the late 1800s, Houston was a typical Texas town, fueled by cotton farming and railroad expansion. Unlike other cities, however, Houston received a major financial and identity boom when oil was discovered at nearby Spindletop in 1901. The oil industry changed Houston forever, with major corporations relocating to the city and using its deep ship channel for distribution.

Houston received another identity change and financial surge in the mid-1900s, when it became a headquarters for the aerospace industry. NASA established its Manned Spacecraft Center in 1961, which eventually became the epicenter of the country's space program with its earth-shattering Gemini and Apollo missions.

With the proliferation of air-conditioning around the same time, Houston's brutal humidity was no longer a year-round deterrent, resulting in corporations and their associated workers relocating from colder climes. The population boomed even more in the 1970s when the Arab Oil Embargo caused Houston's petroleum industry to become one of the most vital assets in the country. The world oil economy in the 1980s caused a recession in Houston, and although the city eventually recovered, it received another black eye in the late 1990s as a result of the Enron accounting fraud scandal.

Texans typically don't consider Houston a viable travel destination, but they should. Most people within the state prefer to visit natural wonders such as Big Bend or South Padre Island, but a dose of cosmopolitan life is good for the soul. Houston's sense of style is a step ahead of the Lone Star State's masses, its restaurants often specialize in the regional cuisine of lesser-known countries (offering tantalizing taste-bud sensations beyond standard eatery fare), and the city's public transportation system is surprisingly comprehensive in its coverage. Incidentally, you'll be able to identify a native by the way they say their city's name—locals don't always pronounce the *H* (resulting in "yoo-ston") for some reason.

A drive through Houston's inner-core neighborhoods reveals what happens when a city doesn't prioritize zoning regulations. Depending on who you ask, it's good (Texans in particular don't like to be told what they can or cannot do with their property) or bad (significant historic neighborhoods and homes are routinely leveled to make room for McMansions). Regardless, it's part of Houston's character, even if that means a 150-year-old home sits in the shadow of a monstrous contemporary house across the street from a gargantuan pseudo-historic retail and residential complex.

Houston may never equal San Antonio in visitation numbers, but its distinctive characteristics—a Southern cosmopolitan city with an independent spirit befitting of Texas—make it a worthy destination for more than just business travelers.

SIGHTS

A city of Houston's size offers countless attractions, most of them cultural in nature. The Museum District is a loose collection (not logically planned, but what in Houston is?) of facilities dedicated to art, science, and children's sites located just southwest of downtown. The urban core features occasional historic buildings and theaters among the modern skyscrapers, and the city boasts several offbeat spots outside of town worth checking out for fun, including the folk-art wonder of the Orange Show, and the historically significant state park featuring the San Jacinto Battleground site and the Battleship *Texas*.

◖ NASA Space Center

Light years away from ordinary cultural attractions is NASA's Space Center (1601 NASA Pkwy., 281/244-2100, www.spacecenter.org, weekdays 10 A.M.–5 P.M., weekends 10 A.M.–6 P.M., extended summer hours, $19.95 adults, $18.95 seniors, $15.95 children ages 4–11). NASA is about as big as it gets for Houston tourist attractions, and it's one of the only cities in the United States to host such a distinct icon of contemporary American history. However, this might not be apparent when you step through the front gates. There

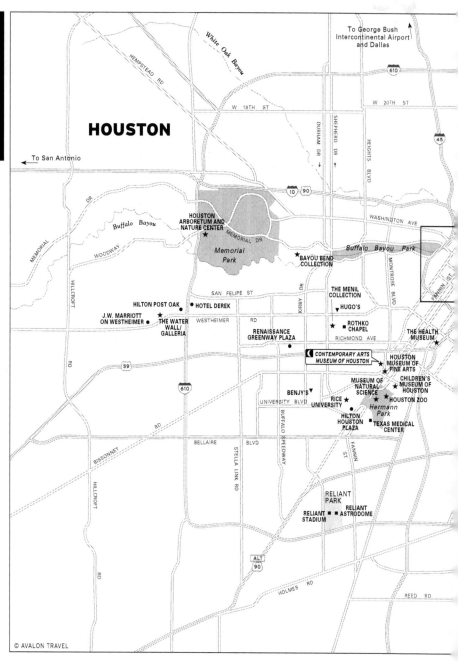

HOUSTON

To San Antonio

To George Bush
Intercontinental Airport
and Dallas

White Oak Bayou

HEMPSTEAD RD

W 18TH ST
W 20TH ST

DURHAM DR
SHEPHERD DR
HEIGHTS BLVD

610
45

MEMORIAL DR

WASHINGTON AVE

Buffalo Bayou

WOODWAY

MEMORIAL

HILLCROFT

10   90

HOUSTON
ARBORETUM AND
NATURE CENTER ★

Memorial
Park

MEMORIAL DR

★ BAYOU BEND
COLLECTION

Buffalo Bayou Park

MONTROSE BLVD

FANNIN ST

SAN FELIPE ST

KIRBY DR

THE MENIL
COLLECTION

▾ HUGO'S

HILTON POST OAK   ● HOTEL DEREK

J.W. MARRIOTT
ON WESTHEIMER ●
★ THE WATER
WALL/
GALLERIA

WESTHEIMER   RD

★ ROTHKO
CHAPEL

THE HEALTH
MUSEUM ■

RENAISSANCE
GREENWAY PLAZA ■

RICHMOND AVE

59

610

UNIVERSITY BLVD

BENJY'S ▾

RICE ★
UNIVERSITY

BUFFALO SPEEDWAY

RD

☾ CONTEMPORARY ARTS
MUSEUM OF HOUSTON

MUSEUM OF
NATURAL
SCIENCE

HOUSTON
MUSEUM OF
FINE ARTS ★

CHILDREN'S
★ MUSEUM OF
HOUSTON

★ HOUSTON ZOO

Hermann
Park

HILTON
HOUSTON
PLAZA ●

TEXAS MEDICAL
CENTER ■

BELLAIRE   BLVD

STELLA LINK RD

FANNIN ST

BISSONNET

HILLCROFT

RD

RELIANT
PARK

RELIANT   ■ ■ RELIANT
STADIUM   ASTRODOME

ALT
90

HOLMES   RD

REED RD

© AVALON TRAVEL

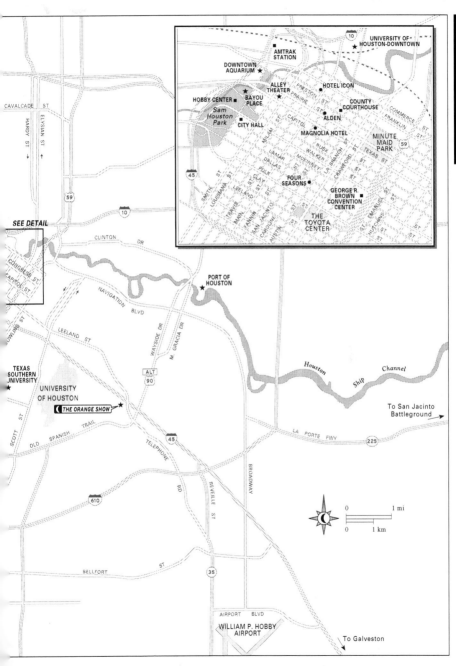

SEE DETAIL

CAVALCADE ST

HARDY ST
ELYSIAN ST

59

10

CLINTON DR

CONGRESS ST
CAPITOL ST

NAVIGATION BLVD

PORT OF
HOUSTON

DOWLING ST

LEELAND ST

WAYSIDE DR
M. GRACIA DR

Houston Ship Channel

TEXAS
SOUTHERN
UNIVERSITY

UNIVERSITY
OF HOUSTON

THE ORANGE SHOW

ALT
90

To San Jacinto
Battleground

SCOTT ST

OLD SPANISH TRAIL

TELEPHONE RD

45

LA PORTE FWY

225

610

REVEILLE ST

BROADWAY

0   1 mi

0   1 km

BELLFORT ST

35

AIRPORT BLVD

WILLIAM P. HOBBY
AIRPORT

To Galveston

Detail map (downtown)

10

UNIVERSITY OF
HOUSTON-DOWNTOWN

AMTRAK
STATION

DOWNTOWN
AQUARIUM

HOBBY CENTER
BAYOU
PLACE

ALLEY
THEATER

HOTEL ICON

COMMERCE ST

Sam
Houston
Park

CITY HALL

COUNTY
COURTHOUSE

FRANKLIN ST

ALDEN

MAGNOLIA HOTEL

MINUTE
MAID
PARK

59

PRESTON ST

PRAIRIE ST

CAPITOL ST

RUSK ST

WALKER ST

MCKINNEY ST

LA BRANCH ST

CRAWFORD ST

TEXAS ST

MILAM ST

LAMAR ST

DALLAS ST

45

POLK ST

CLAY ST

SMITH ST

LOUISIANA ST

TRAVIS ST

LEELAND ST

MAIN ST

FANNIN ST

SAN JACINTO ST

CAROLINE ST

AUSTIN ST

FOUR
SEASONS

GEORGE R.
BROWN
CONVENTION
CENTER

THE
TOYOTA
CENTER

ST EMANUEL ST

HUTCHINS ST

HOUSTON, WE HAVE A LEGACY

Space exploration used to be major international news; now, we hardly know when a mission is taking place. Throughout the past four tumultuous decades, NASA's Johnson Space Center in Houston has been the hub of America's celestial activity.

The facility was established in 1961 as the Manned Spacecraft Center and renamed in honor of former president and Texas native Lyndon B. Johnson in 1973. The Johnson Space Center will forever be associated with its earth-shattering early missions with mighty extraterrestrial names, such as Gemini and Apollo.

The famous Mission Control Center is known as the nerve center of America's human space program, and the facility's remarkable guided tours shed light on the fascinating activities that took place here. Grainy TV footage from the manned Apollo missions comes to life as visitors absorb the significance of being in the same room where the words "The Eagle has landed" and "Houston, we have a problem" were first heard.

For the past decade or so, Mission Control has handled all the activity related to the space shuttle and International Space Station programs. Training for these missions took place at an adjacent building, where astronauts and engineers prepared for their time in orbit by using the Space Vehicle Mockup Facility. This enormous edifice houses space shuttle orbital trainers, an International Space Station trainer, a precision air-bearing floor, and a partial gravity simulator. Although the future of the space program remains unclear, NASA expects to play a role in exploring the outer reaches of our known universe, however that may occur. As of late 2010, Johnson Space Center's workforce consisted of about 3,000 employees, mostly professional engineers and scientists. Of these, approximately 110 are astronauts. For the past 40 years, these men and women have helped humans transcend the physical boundaries of Earth to enhance our knowledge about the universe.

To learn more about Johnson Space Center, visit www.nasa.gov/centers/johnson/home/.

are no time lines or text panels dedicated to the history of America's proud space program; instead, there's a 40-foot-tall playground and exhibits about nature's slimiest animals. At this point it becomes apparent that NASA is about two very distinct experiences: kids and adults. Fortunately, it works well.

Those who want to experience the significance and history of the facility should go directly to the tram tour at the far end of the main building. The open-air tram transports visitors to the space center's significant buildings, including the remarkable Mission Control Center. Here, visitors can learn (or relive) the fascinating saga of the Apollo manned spacecraft missions. A knowledgeable and entertaining guide takes you on a descriptive tour of the extraordinary manned spacecraft experience as you peer through a glass partition at the dated yet iconic original gray-paneled equipment and flat monitor screens.

Goosebumps involuntarily rise on your neck as you realize you're in the exact same room where the words "The Eagle has landed" and "Houston, we have a problem" were first heard. Next door, you'll get to see real astronauts in action at the Space Vehicle Mockup Facility, containing space shuttle orbital trainers, an International Space Station trainer, a precision air-bearing floor, and a partial gravity simulator.

Children may not understand the historical significance of Mission Control, but they'll certainly appreciate Kids Space, a massive collection of exhibits, games, and hands-on activities. Most of NASA's main facility features educational and entertainment-related elements, including an enormous playground for kids, interactive flight simulators for young adults, and the compelling Starship Gallery for all ages, offering life-sized models and an educational effects-filled film.

◖ Contemporary Arts Museum of Houston

As big-city museums go, this is one of the best, with intriguing and captivating (and sometimes head-scratching) objets d'art down every hall. Located in the heart of the Houston Museum District, the CAM (5216 Montrose Blvd., 713/284-8250, www.camh.org, Wed. and Fri. 11 A.M.–7 P.M., Thurs. 11 A.M.–9 P.M., Sat. and Sun. 11 A.M.–6 P.M., free admission) is unmistakable, housed in a distinctive stainless-steel building designed by prominent architect Gunnar Birkerts.

As a noncollecting museum, the facility focuses on current and new directions in art, with regularly changing exhibits and acclaimed education programs. The museum grew steadily in the 1970s and '80s to reach significant status in the nation's art world with celebrated exhibits featuring contemporary still-life painting, thematic installations, performance pieces, and other mediums.

If you're visiting on the last Friday of the month, be sure to drop by the museum's Steel Lounge for an "art"ini while you browse the exhibits and visit the amazing shop, featuring whimsical toys and objects, large posters, decorative items, and exceptional gifts.

Museum of Natural Science

One of the best places in Houston for a family adventure is the science museum (1 Hermann Circle Dr., 713/639-4629, www.hmns.org, Mon.–Sat. 9 A.M.–5 P.M., Sun. 11 A.M.–5 P.M., $15–36 adults, $10–29 seniors and students, based on exhibits). The museum features an almost overwhelming array of exhibits and artifacts covering everything from dinosaurs to gems and minerals to ancient Egypt. Its permanent collection is especially impressive, most notably the Hall of the Americas, with its compelling exhibits depicting the stories of how people arrived on the continent (including Native American, Mayan, and Aztec cultures) and their lifeways once they became permanent residents.

Children will never want to leave the museum's Discovery Place on the lower level,

the Museum of Natural Science

© ANDY RHODES

featuring interactive exhibits dedicated to light and sound waves; machines with levers, pulleys, and gears; and a simulated weather studio. The museum's butterfly exhibit is a bit pricey ($7–8) but worthwhile, especially to see the thousands of colorful, lithe winged creatures peacefully meander throughout the towering domed Mayan rain forest habitat. A lengthy waterfall flows gently in the background, and the butterflies occasionally drop by for a personal visit. The museum also contains a McDonald's, but be forewarned: At lunch and dinner the scene gets about as crazy as Times Square on New Year's Eve.

Houston Museum of Fine Arts

Another Museum District hot spot is the fine arts museum (1001 Bissonnet St., 713/639-7300, www.mfah.org, Tues.–Wed. 10 A.M.–5 P.M., Thurs. 10 A.M.–9 P.M., Fri.–Sat. 10 A.M.–7 P.M., Sun. 12:15 P.M.–7 P.M., $7 adults, $3.50 seniors and students 6–18, free on Thurs.). Billing itself as "the largest art museum in America south of Chicago, west of

Washington, D.C., and east of Los Angeles," the Houston Museum of Fine Arts contains two major buildings offering 300,000 square feet of display space and 18 acres of public gardens drawing more than two million people annually. The museum's collection contains nearly 63,000 pieces of art representing all major continents and dating from antiquity to the present. Highlights include the impressively bold Italian renaissance paintings, the mesmerizing French impressionist works, stunning photographs, vintage jewelry, and renowned works of sculpture.

◖ The Orange Show

You know that occasional burst of inspiration that enters your brain? The one that encourages you to take an idea, no matter how ambitious, and follow through with it? Jeff McKissack, a Houston postman-turned-artist, actually did it. He built an enormous folk-art monument dedicated to oranges. McKissack glorified his favorite fruit with 3,000 square feet of space filled with orange-related folk art now known as The Orange Show (2402 Munger St., 713/926-6368, www.orange-show.org, open most weekends noon–5 P.M., $1). Standing among modest suburban homes just east of downtown Houston, this bizarrely compelling artwork is comprised primarily of brick and concrete, accompanied by metal sculptures, mosaic tilework, and various random objects (birdhouses, windmills, statues). McKissack once delivered oranges throughout the South, and he apparently became obsessed enough with them to fashion this whimsical collection of objects found along his mail route. The absurdity-bordering-on-lunacy factor is rather fascinating, and the devotion to his subject is admirable in a disturbing kind of way. McKissack apparently believed his life work (it took him nearly 25 years to assemble his collection into a publicly accessible venue) would become a major tourist destination, but somehow it never quite caught on with the masses. Regardless, it remains an intriguing folk art environment unlike any other you'll ever encounter.

San Jacinto Battleground–Battleship *Texas* State Historic Sites

Two distinctly different yet remarkably significant historical attractions lie adjacent to each other near the Houston Ship Channel 20 miles east of the city. The San Jacinto Battleground and the Battleship *Texas* (3523 Hwy. 134, 281/479-2431, www.tpwd.state.tx.us) tell the stories of valiant warriors in disparate settings fighting for freedom.

Perhaps most significant to Texas history is the San Jacinto Battleground site, with its remarkable 570-foot-tall monument (15 feet taller than the Washington Monument) commemorating Texas's victory for independence. The 1,200-acre site and its adjoining San Jacinto Museum of History preserve and interpret the legendary battleground where Texian troops under Gen. Sam Houston defeated the Mexican Army in an 18-minute battle on April 21, 1836. The magnificent monument—topped by a 34-foot star symbolizing the Lone Star Republic—is dedicated to the "Heroes of the Battle of San Jacinto and all others who contributed to the independence of Texas."

The ground level houses the San Jacinto Museum of History, containing nearly 400,000 objects, documents, and books spanning 400 years of Texas history. Be sure to watch the fascinating 30-minute movie *Texas Forever! The Battle of San Jacinto*. The site's highlight is the observation deck, a 490-foot-tall vantage point offering stunning sweeping views of the battlefield, ship channel, reflecting pool, and surrounding scenery.

Just across the street lies an important piece of the state's history: the Battleship *Texas*. This impressive 1911 vessel is unique—it's the only remaining battleship to serve in both World Wars I and II and was the first U.S. battleship to mount antiaircraft guns and launch an aircraft.

The mighty ship's multiple decks reveal what life was like for the crew, who bravely defended the stars and stripes during crucial combat situations while enduring overcrowded conditions. The elaborate system of massive guns remains

© ANDY RHODES

the Battleship *Texas*

impressive, and visitors can occupy one of the artillery seats to get a feel for the challenging precision required to operate the heavy machinery. Head below deck to see the cramped cots, officers' quarters, galley, engine room, medical facilities, and other slices of life to get a true appreciation for the distinguished service provided by the men of the *Texas*.

Since the ship has been moored at the site (in the brackish water of the Houston Ship Channel) since 1948, it has experienced significant weakening in its hull. The approval of a 2007 bond package included funds for dry-berthing the ship, expected to be completed in time for its centennial celebration in 2014.

The Health Museum

Since Houston is one of the country's leading medical centers, it makes sense there's a corresponding health museum (1515 Hermann Dr., 713/521-1515, www.mhms.org, Tues.–Sat. 9 A.M.–5 P.M., Sun. noon–5 P.M., $8 adults, $6 seniors and children ages 3–12, occasional fees for traveling exhibits). Located in the Museum District, this modest-sized facility is dedicated to educating visitors (kids, mostly) about the importance of good health. The museum includes one of the best exhibits in town, the Amazing Body Pavilion, where you can experience a human body by walking through it. Start by entering through the mouth and exploring the various systems and organs via innovative interactive displays. Vocal chords, lung capacity, stomach acids, and blood content are portrayed through games, hands-on activities, and informative models. The museum also features traveling exhibits related to children's health issues and a fancy gift shop with fun toys, games, and knickknacks.

Houston Zoo

Consistently rated one of the city's top attractions is the lush, welcoming, and occasionally stinky Houston Zoo (6100 Hermann Park Dr., 713/533-6500, www.houstonzoo. org, daily 9 A.M.–6 P.M., $11 ages 12–64, $7 children ages 2–11, $6 seniors). Five thousand animals keep adults and children entertained

HOUSTON'S HUGE HEALTH CENTER

Houston has become a worldwide destination for people in search of a cure. The **Texas Medical Center,** southwest of downtown, bills itself as the largest medical center in the world.

The sheer size of the complex – 1,000-plus acres (billed as "approximately the same size of Chicago's inside loop") – is impressive, as are the number of patients: 160,000 daily visitors with more than six million annual patient visits.

The medical center's origins date to the 1930s, when businessman Monroe Dunaway Anderson proposed a medical center consisting of hospitals, academic institutions, and support organizations. Land was provided free of charge to institutions as an incentive to build within the complex.

Over the decades, the medical center has flourished, with dozens of facilities and specialists flocking to the enormous complex. It now contains one of the world's highest densities of clinical facilities for patient care and medical research. The center contains 49 medicine-related institutions, including 13 hospitals, 2 medical schools, 4 nursing schools, and several schools for other health-related practices (pharmacy, dentistry, public health, etc.).

In true Texas braggadocio style, the Texas Medical Center proudly touts many of its accomplishments and acumens, including:

- Performs more heart surgeries than anywhere else in the world

- Has delivered 19,500 babies

- Has 21,000 physicians, scientists, researchers, and other advanced degree professionals

- Has 71,500 students, including those in high school, college, and health profession programs

- Has 93,500 employees

- Boasts $7.1 billion in approved building and infrastructure for future growth

---

in 55 acres of various worldwide ecosystems. Be sure to drop by the World of Primates, the Asian Elephant habitat, the lion and tiger exhibit, and the grizzly bear habitat. Kids will also love the Children's Zoo, featuring a petting area with various farm animals, and the "Meet the Keeper" program, offering behind-the-cage insight. Families with children will want to set aside time for a little excursion on the train, which takes a short journey through the park along the zoo's border. Also, if you have children in tow, consider bringing some extra clothes since most kids love the water play area and will undoubtedly get soaked.

Children's Museum of Houston

A must-see if you're in the Museum District with kids is the Children's Museum of Houston (1500 Binz St., 713/522-1138, www.cmhouston.org, Tues.–Sat. 10 A.M.–6 P.M., Thurs. until 8 P.M., Sun. noon–6 P.M., $8 adults and children age 2 and up, $7 seniors). The building itself is a sight to behold—an appropriately playful take on classical architecture with giant colorful details. The fun continues inside, where nine galleries engage children's minds through various subjects including science, geography, performing arts, and history. One of the most popular and informative attractions is the multilevel exhibit How Does It Work? Parents may even pick up a few pointers on how mobile phones function and how turning a key gets an engine running. Younger kids will relish the opportunity to sit in a model car with the freedom to push and pull every button and lever in sight. Other fun activities include an interactive Mexican village, art stations, live shows, and a café with healthy snacks. An added bonus: The Teacher and Family Resource Center has loads of books and items related to child development and parenting for the grown-ups

the playful facade of the Children's Museum of Houston

bathed in natural light. The Menil compound also includes several noteworthy structures near the main museum building. Make time for the octagonal Rothko Chapel and the beautiful Byzantine Fresco Chapel.

The Kemah Boardwalk

Located about 25 miles southeast of downtown on Galveston Bay, the popular Kemah Boardwalk (215 Kipp Ave., 281/535-8100, www.kemahboardwalk.com, open daily, all-day ride passes are available: $20 for adults, $17 for children) features restaurants, shops, fountains, and an impressive collection of amusement-park-style rides at the water's edge. Though it's touristy by nature (and draws suburbanites by the thousands for an escape from their 'hoods), the boardwalk offers a much-needed summertime diversion for families along with a nostalgic sense of fun. The restaurants are more notable for their bayside views than adventurous fare, but there's plenty of excitement nearby in the form of rides—including a bona fide roller coaster, Ferris wheel, and double-decker carousel along with bouncy, swingy, and spinny diversions. Other attractions include a 50,000-gallon aquarium with more than 100 different species of tropical fish, a marvelous meandering train, and an interactive stingray reef.

who may need a break from all the incessant noise and questions.

The Menil Collection

What do you do when you have too much fine art to handle? If you're renowned art collectors John and Dominique de Menil, you open your own museum (1515 Sul Ross St., 713/525-9400, www.menil.org, Wed.–Sun. 11 A.M.–7 P.M., free admission, parking at 1515 W. Alabama St.). Located in the middle of the city's Museum District, the Menil is an ideal place to spend a few hours soaking up some magnificent art spanning many ages. The Menils have passed on, but they left a legacy of approximately 16,000 paintings, sculptures, prints, drawings, photographs, and rare books. Most of the works are modern with an emphasis on the surrealist movement, but there are also African pieces and works from the Byzantine period on display. Be sure to check around each nook and cranny since some of the Menils' most rewarding experiences are in solitary areas where artwork and gardens are

The Water Wall

Houstonians take immense pride in their beloved water wall (2800 Post Oak Blvd., 713/621-8000, weekdays 8 A.M.–6 P.M.). Located southwest of downtown near the Galleria, this six-story structure is exactly what it sounds like—a giant wall of cascading water. But it needs to be experienced to be truly appreciated. The structure is semicircular shaped, and the hypnotic sound of falling water is especially mesmerizing. The gentle mist provides a soothing respite from a hot summer day, and the experience is even cooler at night thanks to the dramatic lighting (and "cooler" temperatures in the 80s). Considered by many to be the most romantic spot in town, the water wall is typically bustling with couples on dates or even getting married. The nearby colossal 64-story-tall Williams/Transco Tower offers a nice urban complement to the scene. Parking can be a hassle—try to snag a spot in the nearby West Drive parking garage, which doesn't charge a fee after 9 P.M. weekdays or on weekends.

Houston Arboretum and Nature Center

Experience Houston's oft-forgotten natural side at the Arboretum and Nature Center (4501 Woodway Dr., 713/681-8433, www.houstonarboretum.org, trails and grounds open daily 7 A.M.–7 P.M., Discovery Room open Tues.–Sun. 10 A.M.–4 P.M., free admission). Located on the west side of near-downtown Memorial Park, the 155-acre nature sanctuary is a green oasis in a city known for its sprawling concrete. Native plants and animals are the focal point, with interactive exhibits and activities educating residents and visitors about the importance of not paving over everything. The park area is beautifully landscaped, and kids will love the Discovery Room's pondering pond and learning tree. Stroll the five miles of trails, hear the sweet sounds of birds, and get a glimpse of Houston's version of the natural world.

Downtown Aquarium

Mingle with marine life at the modestly sized downtown aquarium (410 Bagby St., 713/223-3474, www.aquariumrestaurants.com, Sun.–Thurs. 10 A.M.–9 P.M., Fri.–Sat. 10 A.M.–11 P.M., $9.25 adults, $8.25 seniors, $6.25 children ages 2–12, additional fees for rides and parking). Not as extensive or awe-inspiring as some other big-city aquariums, Houston's version is focused on fun, and there's plenty to be had here. The highlight is the Shark Voyage, where a train takes visitors into a clear tunnel surrounded by blacktips, whitetips, and zebra sharks. Other notable exhibits are the Gulf of Mexico tank with barracuda and snappers, and the Discovery Rig, where kids can get a handle on horseshoe crabs and stingrays. The Ferris wheels (above and below water) are fun, but, like the Shark Voyage, cost a few bucks extra. The aquarium also includes a seemingly unrelated yet interesting exhibit area with several majestic white tigers. Incidentally, the adjacent aquarium restaurant is known for its slow service and mediocre food, so plan accordingly.

Bayou Bend Collection

The affluent home of unfortunately named Ima Hogg, a respected Texas philanthropist,

LITTLE SAIGON, THE SEQUEL

In the 1960s, hundreds of Vietnamese residents fled their country and settled in and around Houston, where they found jobs as fishermen and shrimpers (and working in manufacturing and retail) in a humid coastal environment reminiscent of their homeland. Today, Houston's Vietnamese community of approximately 70,000 is the third largest in the nation, according to U.S. Census figures.

During the past few decades – particularly in the '00s – tens of thousands of Vietnamese residents relocated from California and their native country to purchase homes and open businesses, mostly along a four-mile stretch of Bellaire Boulevard in southwestern Houston. Comparatively cheap housing drew the

Californians, many who lived in Los Angeles's famed Little Saigon district.

Word soon got out that Vietnamese families were selling their pricey L.A. abodes and purchasing homes in Houston for a third of the cost. Their remaining funds were often invested in new Vietnamese-centered enterprise businesses, including restaurants, real estate firms, medical facilities, and supermarkets.

The result is a vibrant community, and its neighboring enclaves – shops and residences representing cultures from Chinese to Latino to Pakistani – add to Houston's cosmopolitan and diverse atmosphere. What was once the Vietnamese "best-kept secret" is quickly becoming a high-profile area.

now houses the Bayou Bend Collection (1 Westcott St., 713/639-7750, www.mfah.org, Tues.–Thurs. 10 A.M.–11:45 A.M., Fri.–Sat. 10 A.M.–11:15 A.M., guided tours $10 adults, $8.50 seniors, $5 students ages 10–17). This spectacular 1928 home is one of Houston's cultural treasures, and it's filled with an impressive collection of nearly 5,000 antique objects showcasing American decorative arts from 1620 to 1870. "Miss Hogg," as she was known, also had a hand in the design of the opulent home and grounds, featuring lush gardens and distinctive decorations spanning from the colonial to antebellum eras. Visitors are encouraged to call in advance to make tour reservations, and it should be noted that children under age 10 are not permitted in the home (apparently some old-fashioned customs are still retained along with the objects).

George Ranch Historical Park

For a step back in time and away from the urban pace, consider a jaunt to George Ranch Historical Park (10215 FM 762 in Richmond, 281/343-0218, www.georgeranch.org, Tues.–Sat. 9 A.M.–5 P.M., $9 adults, $8 seniors, $5 students ages 5–15). Located about 30 miles southeast of downtown near the community of Richmond, the site showcases four generations of family members on a 484-acre living-history site. Visitors discover what life was like for Texans on a working cattle ranch through exhibits and displays at the 1820s pioneer farmstead, an 1890s Victorian mansion, and a 1930s ranch house.

Smaller Museums

The Museum District is rife with attractions, including several smaller museums worth visiting for their focus on a particular aspect of the city's culture. They include the following.

THE BUFFALO SOLDIERS MUSEUM

This museum (1834 Southmore Blvd., 713/942-8920, www.buffalosoldiermuseum.com, Mon.–Fri. 10 A.M.–5 P.M., Sat. 10 A.M.–4 P.M., $5 adults, $3 students) is somewhat small, but its significance is enormous. Its name is derived from the term associated with the African-American troops who served in the U.S. Army and protected the Texas frontier in the late 1800s. The Native Americans reportedly referred to them as Buffalo Soldiers due to their immense bravery and valor. Fittingly, the museum honors the legacy of African-Americans' contributions to military service for the past 150 years. This is a unique collection of materials dedicated to a compelling aspect of Texas and America's heritage. Two stories of exhibits feature artifacts, photos, and maps detailing the importance of legacies being passed on to future generations. It's a true learning experience, and it's inspiring to see the groups of area students making connections with their past as interpretive guides offer insight about the uniforms, flags, and equipment. Note: As of early 2011, the museum was planning to move to a new location yet to be determined. Call in advance regarding its current location.

THE HOLOCAUST MUSEUM

A somber subject is handled admirably at the Holocaust Museum Houston (5401 Caroline St., 713/942-8000, www.hmh.org, Mon.–Fri. 9 A.M.–5 P.M., Sat.–Sun. noon–5 P.M., free admission). The museum's mission is to educate people about the dangers of prejudice and hatred in society, and it certainly makes an impact on everyone who walks through its doors. Visitors learn about the historical and personal stories associated with the Holocaust in the museum's permanent exhibit called Bearing Witness: A Community Remembers, which focuses on the stories of Holocaust survivors living in the Houston area. Displays chronicle the Nazi rise to power and the imprisonment in concentration camps. Artifacts, photos, films, informative panels, and a research library serve as testament to the suffering, with the hope that this educational experience will help prevent future atrocities from occurring.

HOUSTON CENTER FOR PHOTOGRAPHY

One of the best little museums in the region is the Houston Center for Photography (1441

W. Alabama St., 713/529-4755, www.hcponline.org, Wed.–Fri. 11 A.M.–6 P.M., Sat.–Sun. noon–5 P.M., free admission). Located in a funky building at the edge of the Museum District, the HCP's mission is to encourage and educate people about art and photography. Exhibits showcase local and national photographers, and programs and services strive to stimulate dialogue about the art form through digital workstations, presentations about methods and critique, and community collaboration.

ENTERTAINMENT AND EVENTS

The Urban Cowboy legend was born in Houston in the early 1980s, and in some parts of town, it's never left. Visitors can get a good feel for the true (and tired) honky-tonks by sampling a few of the city's many nightlife options. Houston has a healthy blues scene, and the bars and dance clubs are reminders of the city's cosmopolitan culture. Speaking of culture, the performing arts in Houston are truly befitting of the nation's fourth-largest city, particularly its internationally renowned opera and ballet companies and spectacular symphony.

Performing Arts

THE HOUSTON GRAND OPERA

A big-time city deserves a big-time opera company, and Houston has one in The Houston Grand Opera (713/228-6737, www.houstongrandopera.org). Performances are held at the downtown Wortham Theater Center (501 Texas Ave.), and the opera is considered one of the city's cultural crown jewels. It's the only opera company on the planet to win a Tony, two Emmys, and two Grammy awards, and it has a reputation for commissioning and performing new works, with dozens of world premieres in more than 50 years. The company tours extensively, bringing productions to Europe, Japan, and Egypt, and on the home front, it's been lauded for its accessibility (tickets for some shows start at $15, and the casual dress series is popular among the younger crowd).

THE HOUSTON BALLET

Another world-class performing arts company is The Houston Ballet (713/523-6300, www.houstonballet.org). Also utilizing the beautiful Wortham Theater Center, the ballet has developed a national reputation for making stars of principal dancers and staging contemporary, edgy ballets. In recent years, the company has been an important diplomat for the city by taking its impressive show on the road to China, London, Canada, and Washington, D.C.'s Kennedy Center.

THE HOUSTON SYMPHONY

Also highly respected in the city's performing arts scene is The Houston Symphony (713/224-4240, www.houstonsymphony.org). The symphony has been impressing audiences at the magnificent downtown Jones Hall (615 Louisiana St.) for more than four decades, and it currently performs more than 170 concerts attended by nearly 350,000 people annually. Shows include a classical season, pops series, *Messiah* performances at Christmas, and family concerts. In the summer, the symphony performs outdoor shows and stages children's performances throughout the region.

THEATER

Houston boasts several high-quality theater companies, but two consistently emerge as the top of the playbill. The **Alley Theatre** (615 Texas Ave., 713/220-5700, www.alleytheatre.org) stages its productions in a facility that's a sight to behold—a medieval-type fortress in the heart of downtown separated into two stages. The Alley is known and respected throughout Houston for its ability to embrace the old and the new. Their classic and contemporary performances consistently draw wide audiences. Also drawing rave reviews is the **Ensemble Theatre** (3535 Main St., 713/520-0055, www.ensemblehouston.com). Billed as the largest African-American professional theater company in the country with its own productions and facility, the Ensemble regularly stages acclaimed dramas, comedies, and musicals for enthusiastic crowds. The company also runs an educational touring program and a popular summer training program for youth.

Live Music
BLUES
Mention blues towns and most people think of Memphis or Chicago, but Houston definitely belongs in the mix. It has a long-standing tradition of serving up swampy bayou blues, and some of the state's grittiest and most soulful players have emerged from the city's downtown African-American neighborhoods. One of the best places to see them play is the legendary **Etta's Lounge** (5120 Scott St., 713/528-2611). You'll have to seek Etta's out since there's no sign out front, a testament to its unassuming vibe. Inside, you'll find the real deal—a no-frills, cavernous room allowing the focus to be on the stage. The refreshingly diverse clientele isn't there to be seen (just to hear). Etta's shines on Sunday nights, when Grady Gaines wows the crowd with his soulful sax. Bring your appetite for a tasty meal, too, since Etta's serves some fine soul food in the restaurant up front.

The **Continental Club** (3700 Main St., 713/529-9899, www.continentalclub.com) doesn't stage blues exclusively—roots and alternative rock acts are often on the bill—but the local and touring blues bands that play here are typically the best around. An offshoot of the legendary Austin venue, Houston's version of the Continental is appropriately more sprawling but still dedicated to offering some of the most soulful music in Bayou City. Bring your dancing shoes, since patrons often shake a leg to work off their meal.

COUNTRY AND WESTERN
Houston is the true home of the Urban Cowboy, so grab those boots if you're fixin' to head out for some two-steppin' at one of these fine dance halls. For a real-deal honky-tonk experience, go straight to **Blanco's** (3406 W. Alabama St., 713/439-0072). Located near downtown just north of the Rice University area, Blanco's is small in size but huge on character. Some of the best live acts in the state play

here, and there's always a fascinating array of couples gliding across the dance floor, from old-school octogenarians to new-school college students. The music is classic country, transporting all ages to a bygone era of bolo ties and beehive hairdos.

Less charming yet more appealing to the masses are the city's big-box country music venues. Located near the Galleria among the trendy upscale dance clubs is the refreshingly unhip **Firehouse Saloon** (5930 Southwest Frwy., 713/977-1962, www.firehousesaloon. com). There's some flashiness here—big ol' shiny belt buckles, fancy light machines, Vegas-style video games—but the crowd is genuinely friendly. Although cover bands take the stage most nights, you'll find the occasional worthy local band looking to catch their big break.

For an overwhelming dose of Lone Star State culture, drop by the **Big Texas Dance Hall and Saloon** (803 E. NASA Blvd., 281/461-4400, www.bigtexassaloon.com). It's a bit hokey—the decor is pseudo-rustic with cacti and Western "artifacts"—but the scene is vibrant, especially for singles. Live music is the big draw on Thursday, when regional acts get boots scootin', but DJs fill the dance floor most weekends.

JAZZ
One of the many benefits of being a music fan in a big city is access to quality jazz clubs. Houston is a major player on the jazz circuit, and it's a hotbed for some of the genre's rising stars. The stalwart on the scene is **Sambuca** (909 Texas Ave., 713/224-5299, www.sambucarestaurant.com). Located in the stunning historic Rice Hotel, Sambuca is a jazz fan's dream—a classy downtown venue offering nightly performances from local and national performers. Accompany your ideal evening with a juicy steak from the acclaimed restaurant and a postmeal or set-break visit to the cigar room.

For a truly intimate experience, visit **Cezanne** (4100 Montrose Blvd., 713/522-9621, www.blacklabradorpub.com), a 40-seat venue in the trendy Montrose district. Cezanne's is considered Houston's premier jazz club, which is nice for the aficionados who get a chance to sit merely feet away from national acts but unfortunate for the hundreds or even thousands of other music lovers who'd like to see the show. Regardless, every seat in this cozy spot is a good one, and you'll hear, see, and feel every note being played.

CONCERT VENUES

Since Houston is such a business- and convention-oriented city, visitors often find themselves in town for a few days in search of familiar rock acts or with an expense account to afford some pricey tickets. Virtually every touring act makes a stop in Houston, so out-of-towners also have an opportunity to catch shows that may not make it to their home turf until the second or third leg of the tour. These folks will likely want to browse the online calendar for the downtown entertainment complex **Bayou Place** (500 Texas St., 713/227-0957, www.bayouplace.com). The Bayou's **Verizon Wireless Theater** (713/230-1600, www.verizonwirelesstheater.com) covers the gamut from rock and country to comedy and musicals, while the adjacent **Hard Rock Cafe** (713/227-1392, www.hardrock.com) offers its venerable blend of music and memorabilia. Nearby is the more club-oriented **Rocbar** (713/236-1100, www.rocbartx.com), where DJs and live acts keep the party going until 2 A.M.

If you still want to rock but prefer to roll away from the hassle of downtown, head to the classic Houston venue **Fitzgerald's** (2706 White Oak Dr., 713/862-3838, www.fitzlivemusic.com). Housed in an enormous historic Polish dance hall, Fitz's features indie rock acts, classic Americana groups, and comfy local bands. The all-ages policy can rub some old-timers the wrong way, but they can always escape to the spacious back patio for a fresh breath of smoky air. Also housed in a historical venue is the folky **Anderson Fair** (2007 Grant St., 713/528-8576, www.andersonfair.com). This tucked-away club in the Montrose area has been hosting up-and-coming folk and roots rock acts for decades and continues to stage

some of Texas's most popular Americana acts. Note: Anderson Fair is only open on weekends and only accepts cash.

Bars and Clubs
BARS

One of the most popular spots to open in the past several years is **Max's Wine Dive** (4720 Washington Ave., 713/880-8737, www.maxswinedive.com). "Dive" is a misnomer, since the trendy locale caters to an upscale clientele, but the pairings of drink and food are incredibly down 'n' dirty. You never realized a glass of red wine would complement a burger so well. Or a flute of champagne with fried chicken. More than 150 wines are available by the glass or bottle, and wines are available to go. An added bonus: Most of the beverages and food are Texas organic products. Max's was spawned from the outstanding Uptown establishment **The Tasting Room** (1101 Uptown Park Blvd., 713/993-9800, www.tastingroomwines.com), a big hit with the hip oenophiles (wine aficionados) who frequent the place. The amazing Wine Wall offers hundreds of options for less than $30, or you can descend to the cellar for the more expensive varieties. Drop a $6 corking fee, and you can sip your purchase on-site. Much like its son Max's, The Tasting Room offers perfect pairings of wine and food, including cheeses, olives, salamis, tapas, and pizzas.

One of the more distinctive spots in town to grab a cocktail is **Dean's Credit Clothing** (314 Main St., 713/227-3326, www.deanshouston.com). Nope, that's not a misprint. Housed inside a historic downtown 1930s clothing store, Dean's strives to maintain a much of its early charm as possible. Original features include the elevator (one of the first in Texas), the ornate flooring, and checkout area that's been transformed into a bar. Even the clothing racks remain stocked with vintage items, available for purchase at the bar. Local fashion shows are held here on occasion, and best of all, the drink prices are almost as dated as the surroundings—$2 for cans of Pabst Blue Ribbon and $5 well drinks. Nearby is the low-key and comfy **Warren's Inn** (307 Travis St., 713/247-

9207). A longtime downtown lounge, Warren's is a dark and mellow place where the regulars look like they've occupied their spots at the bar for decades. Be sure to check out the jukebox with appropriate soundtrack music from the 1940s to 1960s.

Many Houston residents associate pub crawls with the **Rice Village** area, where a collection of English-style brewpubs has kept nearby university students out of libraries for decades. The following locales are ideal spots for grabbing a freshly poured pint, finding the jukebox of your dreams, and soaking up the freewheeling college scene: **The Ginger Man** (5607 Morningside Dr., 713/526-2770, www.gingermanpub.com), **Hans' Bier Haus** (2523 Quenby St., 713/520-7474, www.hansbierhaus.com, be sure to play some bocce ball out back), and **Two Rows Restaurant & Brewery Pub** (2400 University Blvd., 713/529-2739, www.tworows.com).

CLUBS

Like most metropolitan areas, Houston's club scene is an ever-changing animal, leaping from spot to spot with an unpredictable life span. One that's managed to stay alive for a while is **Grasshopper** (506 Main St., 713/222-1442, www.grasshopperhouston.com). Located in a swanky late-1800s downtown building, Grasshopper has an Amsterdam vibe, with two separate areas—one for dancing and one for lounging. The thumping hip-hop and R&B tracks keep people jumping on the dance floor, and the alcoves offer a safe escape from the hordes. Just a few blocks away is **Club Venue** (719 Main St., 713/236-8150, www.venuehouston.com). Locals have been lining up here for years to dance the night away to über-trendy house and techno beats. Call in advance for bottle service or to reserve a VIP table.

The appropriately named **Next** (2020 McKinney St., 713/221-8833, www.whatsnexthouston.com) is one of the city's up-and-coming spots where eager line-waiters clamor to be next in line. Located in an obscure building in the city's Warehouse District, the club feels like an L.A. or NYC hot spot with its elevated dance floor, shiny DJ booth, and glass box of beautiful dancers above the bar. Those not as interested in keeping up with the latest trends or worrying about specifically appropriate footwear should head to **La Carafe** (813 Congress St., 713/229-9399). Known for its laid-back vibe and legendary jukebox, La Carafe is in a historic brick building that exudes character. Order some wine, punch in a little Otis Redding on the jukebox, and settle in for a long and cozy evening.

It would be a downright shame to not include a country and western venue in Houston's club listings, so if you're up for some line dancing or people watching head 'em up to **Wild West** (6101 Richmond Ave., 713/266-3455, www.wildwesthouston.com, closed Mon. and Tues). Though it's a bit huge for a club, there's plenty to see and do here, including soaking up the Urban Cowboy scene and even taking dance lessons (offered for just $3 on Sunday afternoons).

GAY BARS

Houston has perhaps the largest gay scene in the South, and most of it is centered on the city's Montrose District west of downtown. This is where most of the gay bars are, drawing all walks of life, from the understated to the overblown. One of the newer clubs on the scene is **JR's** (808 Pacific St., 713/521-2519, www.jrsbarandgrill.com), drawing a semiprofessional crowd for drink specials, karaoke, and male dancers. Parking is hard to come by, so consider using the valet service across the street at the old-school (and somewhat outdated) **Montrose Mining Company** (805 Pacific St., 713/529-7488). Next door to JR's is the popular **South Beach** (810 Pacific St., 713/529-7623, www.southbeachthenightclub.com), a hot spot for dancing. South Beach attracts a primarily gay clientele, but everyone is welcome on the dance floor, where suspended jets spray liquid ice on the crowd to keep things cool. A bit farther away, yet still in the Montrose area, is **EJ's** (2517 Ralph St., 713/527-9071, www.ejsbar.com). Pool is a popular draw here, as are the cheap drinks and a second-floor martini bar.

Events

WINTER

Each year in mid-January, the Antioch Missionary Baptist Church of Christ hosts the **Gardere Martin Luther King Jr. Oratory Competition** (713/867-3286) in honor of Dr. Martin Luther King Jr. The event also includes a highly anticipated performance by the Salvation Army Choir. In mid-February, the **Texas Home and Garden Show** (800/654-1480) offers interactive displays and more than 1,500 exhibitors at the Reliant Center to help Houstonians and visitors get their spring gardening plans growing.

SPRING

Every March, the University of Texas Health Science Center presents the popular **Brain Night at the Museum** (713/521-1515), featuring presentations about how the brain works, a gross yet fascinating dissection of a sheep's brain, an informative video, and other brainy activities. In April, don't miss the **Bayou City Cajun Fest** (281/890-5500) at Traders Village. Patrons enjoy crawfish, po'boys, zydeco bands, and all kinds of Cajun culture. Another popular annual springtime event is the **Asian Pacific Heritage Festival** (713/784-1112), featuring an impressive parade, food booths, and cultural activities at the Alief Community Park in southwest Houston each May.

SUMMER

It gets downright sweltering in Houston during the summer months, but that doesn't deter locals from celebrating. One of the city's best-known annual events is **Juneteenth** (713/558-2600), commemorating the day in June that enslaved Texans learned about their freedom via the Emancipation Proclamation. Juneteenth activities include national gospel, blues, and jazz acts taking the stage at Hermann Park, along with plenty of good eats and revelry. Paper-folding aficionados won't want to miss the annual **Origami Festival at Tansu** (713/880-5100), held each July in Houston Heights. Participate in the interactive workshops, exhibits, and demonstrations.

September is still the height of the summer in Houston, and residents celebrate by enjoying hot jazz at the **Houston International Jazz Festival** (713/839-7000). Let the smooth sounds of local and nationally known jazz artists provide a cool breeze to beat the September heat.

FALL AND HOLIDAY

Get your ghoul on with the city's annual **Ghost Walks** (713/222-9255) throughout October. Hauntees ride on the Metro to different downtown locales where they can get freaked out by various urban legends and authentic historical death scenes. Speaking of deceased, locals and visitors descend en masse on downtown neighborhoods on November 2 as part of the **Day of the Dead Festival** (713/343-0218). Parades and festivals honor the former lives of family and friends. In early December, City Hall becomes the gathering place for **Chanukah Fest** (713/774-0300). The Chabad Lubavitch Outreach of Houston sponsors this annual event featuring traditional food, live music, craft demonstrations, and holiday activities.

SHOPPING

Downtown

Several years ago, the big news in Houston's downtown shopping scene was the transfer from Foley's to **Macy's** (1110 Main St., 713/405-7035, www.macys.com) in the venerable five-story department store in the heart of the historic business district. The building housed the original Foley Bros. store, an establishment that went on to become a mall mainstay across the country. Now that it's been in place for a few years, Macy's ably continues the tradition of offering quality clothing, perfume, and accessories in a cosmopolitan environment. For a real urban experience, take the Metro to the Main Street rail stop and step out near Macy's grand front doors.

Another popular downtown shopping destination is the pleasantly modest **Shops at Houston Center** (1200 McKinney St., 713/759-1442, www.shopsathc.com), comprised of nearly 50 specialty stores and boutiques beneath a canopy-style atrium. Look for jewelry, home decor items, and a quick bite to eat as you stroll the two-block complex among meandering visitors and bee-lining professionals. The shops are connected to Houston's bizarre yet fascinating **Downtown Tunnels** (713/650-3022, tour info at 713/222-9255, www.downtownhouston.com), a six-mile system of air-conditioned subterranean walkways. More than 82 downtown buildings are linked via the tunnels, which started as a small system to connect three downtown theaters in the 1930s. Now, tunnelers can find scores of services, ranging from banks to restaurants to clinics to clothing boutiques, 20 feet below the surface. The tunnel system is accessible from street-level stairwells, and elevators and escalators inside buildings situated above the passageways. The only building offering direct access to the tunnels from the street is the Wells Fargo Plaza (1000 Louisiana St.).

Uptown

One of the city's most popular tourist and shopping destinations is the colossal **Galleria** (5085 Westheimer Rd., 713/622-0663, www.galleriahouston.com). This city within a city—the fourth-largest mall in the country—draws more than 24 million visitors annually. Noted for its remarkable glass atriums and suspended balconies, the Galleria contains a popular ice-skating rink, two Westin hotels, and more than 375 shops, including top-notch retailers such as Nordstrom (the only location in Houston), Saks Fifth Avenue, Neiman Marcus, Cartier, Gucci, and Tiffany & Co. The best time to experience the Galleria is Saturday afternoon. It's an absolute madhouse, and you probably won't get much shopping done, but the people watching is the best the city has to offer. Grab a latte and keep an eye out for the Hispanic girls in their flashy gowns celebrating their Quinceaneras (a cultural rite of passage dedicated to a girl's 15th birthday).

Across the street is the slightly more eclectic **Centre at Post Oak** (5000 Westheimer Rd.), offering a good mix of corporate giants and smaller independent stores. Barnes & Noble and Marshalls peacefully coexist alongside specialty shops such as J. Tiras Classic Handbags & Jewelry and Jeffrey Stone Ltd. Upscale dining options are also a part of this pedestrian-friendly environment.

Nearby is the charming **Uptown Park** (1400 Post Oak Blvd., 713/850-1400, www.uptownparkhouston.com). Billed as "Houston's Italian-style piazza," Uptown Park features pleasant European-esque buildings, lush landscaped walkways, and soothing fountains. Coffee shops, upscale clothing retailers, fancy jewelry stores, and luxury spas add to the ambience.

Rice Village-Kirby District

Aside from the Galleria, one of Houston's most popular and venerable shopping destinations is **Rice Village** (Rice Blvd. and Kirby Dr. just west of Rice University, www.ricevillageonline.com). This 16-block complex has been a favorite place for bargain hunting, browsing, and people watching since the 1930s. The Village features scores of independent shops and eclectic boutiques along with local restaurants and services, some located in historic homes, others in modest 1950s strip centers. The nearby **Highland Village** (4055 Westheimer Rd., 713/850-3100, www.shophighlandvillage.com) is considered a more subdued version of the galleria. It's an upscale collection of shops, but the stucco buildings and breezy palm trees give it a more relaxed feel than other high-end plazas. Home furnishings are big here, including retail giants such as Williams-Sonoma, Crate & Barrel, and Restoration Hardware, along with dozens of fancy clothing stores and restaurants.

Southwest Houston

An eclectic mix of Asian shops and restaurants awaits on **Harwin Drive,** roughly between Gessner and Fondren Streets. The area offers an epic mash-up of typical American suburban sprawl (strip malls, gaudy signs) and cultural diversity (Thai, Pakistani, Indian, and Chinese vendors, authentic eateries). Plan to spend an afternoon browsing for unexpected gems and bargain clothes, accessories, furniture, and knickknacks. Just a couple miles west on Harwin is **Chinatown,** a concentrated collection of Chinese establishments, including a mall with bookstores, music, gifts, and cooking items.

Katy Outlet Stores

Located about 25 miles west of Houston is the immensely popular **Katy Mills** (5000 Katy Mills Cir., 281/644-5015, www.katymills. com), a destination for bargain hunters who thrive on finding discounted clothing and products from big-time retailers. Katy Mills goes a step beyond other outlet malls, however, by including a 20-screen movie theater, a merry-go-round, and rock wall. It's the brand-name stores that offer the true thrills, however, including Tommy Hilfiger, Off 5th Saks Fifth Avenue, Books-A-Million, Bass Pro Shops, Last Call Neiman Marcus, Cole Haan, and Polo Ralph Lauren.

SPORTS AND RECREATION

Houston is home to several professional sports franchises as well as myriad opportunities for year-round outdoor activities, including golf, hiking, and biking. Pro sports teams are the big draw, especially since so many Houston residents are transplants from other parts of the country in search of opportunities to see their hometown heroes on the field. Natives have had reason to jump on the bandwagon for several sports, most notably the Astros baseball team and Rockets basketball squad, both with postseason appearances in the past decade.

Professional Sports

Houston is a football town, but since the relatively new Houston Texans have been rather punchless since their inception, sports fans are drawn to the venerable (by this city's standards) **Houston Astros.** In 1965, the Astros became the primary occupants of the then-futuristic Astrodome, referred to as the Eighth Wonder of the World. Indeed, it was a sight to behold and an especially welcome respite from Houston's horrendous humidity. The Astros assembled some worthy teams in the 1980s,

© ANDY RHODES

the Astrodome, a.k.a. the Eighth Wonder of the World

most notably with hometown hero Nolan Ryan, and two decades later, they attained similar success with another local legend at the helm, Roger Clemens, and a powerhouse offense featuring the "Killer Bs"—Craig Biggio, Jeff Bagwell, and Lance Berkman. By this time, the Astros had fled the Eighth Wonder for the comfy confines of the downtown Minute Maid Park (501 Crawford St.), a classic urban ball field with a modern retractable roof. For Astros ticket and schedule information, contact the team at www.houston. astros.mlb.com or 713/259-8000.

Once home to the storied Houston Oilers football franchise (before they bolted for Tennessee and became the Titans), the city is now the home to the NFL's **Houston Texans.** As an expansion team, the Texans were slow to gain their footing in the NFL, and despite passing on hometown hero and University of Texas standout quarterback Vince Young with their number-one draft pick in 2006, the Texans are building a formidable franchise that, regardless of their spot in the standings, continues to draw substantial crowds to Reliant Stadium (1 Reliant Park). For Texans ticket and schedule information, contact the team at www.houstontexans.com or 832/667-2000.

Basketball isn't as big a draw in Texas as other sports, but the **Houston Rockets** have always had a considerable following. Their successful 1990s teams, featuring top-notch talent such as Clyde "The Glide" Drexler and Hakeem "The Dream" Olajuwon, were the talk of the NBA during their glory years, when they won the NBA title in 1993 and '94. Though they've been less threatening lately, they boast Yao Ming, a 7-foot, 6-inch-tall superstar from China who draws a sizable international fan base. The Rockets hold court at the downtown Toyota Center (1510 Polk St.). For ticket and schedule information, contact www.nba.com/rockets or 713/627-3865.

Parks

Most big cities have a showcase central park offering an inviting natural oasis among the harsh urban environs. Houston's version is **Hermann Park** (6001 Fannin St., 713/524-5876, www.houstontx.gov). Located in the heart of the Museum District just southwest of downtown, Hermann Park is a 400-acre magnet for joggers, dog walkers, bikers, and families in search of some rare green space in a city known for its rampant development. Trails and trees are abundant here, as are the amenities and services, including a theater, golf course, and garden center. The park is filled with statues, too; look for monuments to Sam Houston, Mahatma Gandhi, and namesake George Hermann.

Farther outside of town but worth the 30-minute drive is **Armand Bayou Nature Center** (8500 Bay Area Blvd. in Pasadena, 281/474-2551, www.abnc.org, Tues.–Sat. 9 A.M.–5 P.M., Sun. noon–5 P.M., $3 adults, $1 seniors and students ages 4–12). Located near NASA on the west side of Galveston Bay, the nature center offers residents and visitors a chance to learn about native plant and animal species, hike on the discovery trails, or see the live animal displays featuring the likes of

bison, hawks, and spiders. The main area of the park contains a boardwalk traversing the marshes and forests, and providing a glimpse of the beautiful bayou region of East Texas. The best way to experience this natural wonder is by boat—consider taking a tour on the Bayou Ranger pontoon boat or signing up for a guided canoe tour.

Hiking and Biking

Rivaling Hermann Park for crown jewel of Houston's public green space is **Memorial Park** (6501 Memorial Dr., 713/845-1000, www.houstontx.gov, daily 6 A.M.–11 P.M.). What sets Memorial Park apart are its recreational facilities, primarily the hike and bike trails. Located on 1,400 acres formerly dedicated to World War I–era Camp Logan, Memorial Park is now a magnet for all varieties of athletes and exercisers.

The three-mile Seymour Lieberman Exercise Trail is popular with residents who have a daily workout routine and utilize the exercise stations and restrooms along the route. More dedicated runners use the nearby asphalt timing track to work on speed and develop skills, while the Memorial Park Picnic Loop offers a smooth surface for in-line skaters, traditional roller skate enthusiasts, and hikers. Dogs are welcome and even encouraged at the park— canine drinking fountains are conveniently located at ground level along the jogging trails. Just remember to keep your pooch on a leash and to bring a doggie bag.

Mountain bikers race to the park for the miles of challenging terrain along the Buffalo Bayou. The southwest section of the park contains color-coded trails with maps at the trailheads, and Infantry Woods provides an advanced trail for those with superior skills. The park's other recreational opportunities include a full-service tennis center, swimming pool, golf course, fitness center, baseball diamonds, a croquet field, and sand volleyball courts.

Just east of Memorial Park is the pleasantly modest-sized **Buffalo Bayou Park** (1800 Allen Pkwy., 713/845-1000, www.buffalobayou.org), an urban greenbelt with the namesake waterway as its centerpiece. With the towering Houston skyline as a backdrop, the park draws bikers, joggers, art lovers, and walkers from across the city who relish its riverside trails and bustling activity. In addition to the smooth, wide trail system, the 124-acre park contains exercise stations, a recreation center, disc golf course, children's playground, and popular dog recreation area. Public art abounds along the jogging trail, from stainless-steel objects representing tree roots on an overpass to the large stone-blocks-turned-sculpture that remain from the city's demolished civic auditorium. Visit the park's website to download PDFs of trail maps.

Golf

Houston's Parks and Recreation Department (www.houstontx.gov) runs seven respectable municipal golf courses, a worthy city service in an urban environment that features year-round moderate temperatures and developers ready to capitalize on any available open space. Three of the most popular courses are located within the loop, drawing golfers and hackers to the links' well-maintained grounds and affordable greens fees.

The gem of the downtown-area muni courses is **Memorial Park Golf Course** (1001 E. Memorial Loop Dr., 713/862-4033), a 600-acre oasis of rolling fairways and challenging greens. Originally constructed as a nine-hole sand green course for soldiers at Camp Logan (now Memorial Park), the links feature lush landscapes, putting and chipping greens, a golf museum, contemporary clubhouse, and always-packed driving range offering shade and lighting.

Located adjacent to the city's Museum District, **Hermann Park Golf Course** (2155 Cambridge St., 713/526-0077) is another natural escape from the surrounding urban scenery. Lengthy fairways, snug out-of-bounds, and occasional water hazards make Hermann a favorite among serious golfers, who appreciate the shade of the ancient oaks and steady surface of the Bermuda-grass greens. While at the turn, be sure to order a hot dog or two from the clubhouse kitchen.

Farther south of town is **Wortham Park Golf Course** (7000 Capitol St., 713/928-4260), a former private course now operated by the city. The sportiest of the three downtown-area courses, Wortham Park features hilly terrain, tight turns, and several short par fours. The course also offers a practice green and bunker, a chipping green, and a full driving range.

ACCOMMODATIONS
Downtown
$100-150

One of the best ways to experience Houston—at an affordable rate, no less—is at the fabulous **◖ Magnolia Hotel** (1100 Texas Ave., 713/221-0011 or 888/915-1110, www.magnoliahotel-houston.com, $143 d). This historic downtown gem hosts many business guests and events, and the bustling activity adds to the cosmopolitan aura of the grand 1926 building. The Magnolia offers an impressive number of complimentary services, including wireless Internet access, downtown car transportation, a continental breakfast, and, even better: free happy hour drinks and milk and cookies at bedtime. The rooftop fitness center, lap pool, and hot tub make the Magnolia one of Houston's top-notch lodging options.

At the complete opposite end of the chronological scale is the eco- and tech-minded **Westin Houston Vintage Park** (14555 Vintage Preserve Pkwy., 281/379-7300, www.starwoodhotels.com, $113 d). Part of a "lifestyle center" in the bustling northwestern part of town, Element touts its environmentally friendly design and construction, as well as its thorough provision of widespread wireless access for computers, phones, and portable online devices. Other amenities include a hot breakfast, open-flow guest rooms with fully equipped kitchens, and an evening reception (Monday–Thursday 6–7:30 P.M.) with hand-selected regional wines and beers, soft drinks, and appetizers.

$150-200

For a deluxe downtown lodging experience in

a major city of Houston's size, it doesn't get much better than the **Alden** (the former Sam Houston Hotel at 1117 Prairie St., 832/200-8800, www.aldenhotels.com, $150 d). The Alden offers near-luxury accommodations without charging outrageous prices. Pamper yourself in this contemporary setting with amenities such as fancy bathrooms (granite walls and glass-walled showers with plush robes and towels), quality bedding (400-thread-count sheets, down comforters and pillows, pillowtop mattresses), as well as DVD libraries, gourmet snacks, a minibar, and free Wi-Fi service.

For a modest price increase, consider **Hilton Americas** (1600 Lamar St., 713/739-8000, www.hilton.com, $167 d), a humongous hotel with more than 1,200 rooms towering over downtown. This is a big-time business destination since the Hilton is attached to the convention center, but weekends are a nice (and cheaper) time to stay since the hotel's many amenities are even more accessible. Highlights include three restaurants, several bars and lounges, and an impressive spa and health club with downtown views. Rooms feature free wireless Internet access, fancy linens (300 thread count), and an in-room refreshment center.

Another worthwhile option is the clean and spacious **Best Western Downtown Inn and Suites** (915 W. Dallas St., 713/571-7733, www.bestwestern.com, $159 d). Rooms and suites include microwaves, fridges, and free Wi-Fi service, and the hotel offers a free full breakfast every morning, happy hour cocktails (Monday–Thursday), a fitness center, spa, and outdoor pool.

Those seeking the comforts of home in a historic urban setting will enjoy the **Residence Inn Houston Downtown** (904 Dallas St., 832/366-1000, www.marriott.com, $169 d). The building itself is spectacular—the 1921 Humble Oil Building features well-restored Classical Revival details such as brass elevator doors, tall ceilings, and stately rose marble. Hotel amenities include free Internet access, free drinks at the evening social hour, a large pool, fitness center, and spacious suites with fully equipped kitchens and separate sleeping and living areas. Check out this over-the-top service: You can leave a grocery list at the front desk and return in the evening to a stocked kitchen.

$200-250

Sometimes a visit to a cosmopolitan city requires a cosmopolitan lodging experience. In Houston, look no further than the 🄲 **Hotel Icon** (220 Main St., 713/224-4266, www.hotelicon.com, $219 d), offering dynamic contemporary lodging in the heart of downtown. This 12-story hotel is filled with bold colors and lavish details, including marble countertops, antique claw-foot tubs, luxury robes, and plush linens. In the mood for a bubble bath? Simply summon the Bath Butler for a perfectly drawn sudsy experience. Other amenities include free Wi-Fi service, Web TV, a stocked minibar, and fresh-cut flowers.

If a historic setting is more your style, consider the elegant **Lancaster** (701 Texas St., 713/228-9500, www.thelancaster.com, $219 d), considered Houston's original small luxury hotel. The Lancaster's posh aura is immediately apparent upon entering the lobby, decorated with large oil paintings, beveled glass, and dramatic lighting. There's a sense of European opulence in the hotel's decor, and the guest rooms capture this charm with dark wood two-poster beds, feather pillows and duvets, and brass furnishings. The Lancaster also offers free wireless Internet service, plush bathrobes, and free car service to nearby attractions.

$250 AND ABOVE

Those in search of five-star accommodations have several downtown options, including the reliably luxurious **Four Seasons** (1300 Lamar St., 713/650-1300, www.fourseasons.com, $275 d). The skyline views are outstanding here, as are the services, including the exquisite spa and salon, a spacious pool and fitness center, complimentary downtown car service, a tasty antipasti bar, and rooms featuring plush bathrobes, minibars, and Wi-Fi access. Some of the most expensive lodging in town is at the mediocre-sounding **Inn at the Ballpark** (1520 Texas St., 713/228-1520, www.innattheball-park.com, $279 d), located within earshot of the cracks of the Houston Astros' bats. The location is one of the prime amenities here, since the other services (aside from being five-star in quality) are as inspiring as the hotel's name. The Inn at the Ballpark offers free transportation services around town as well as complimentary Internet access and a light breakfast.

Uptown
$50-100
Some of the best bargains in the city are in the busy Uptown area west of downtown near the Galleria. Among them are **Drury Inn and Suites** (1615 W. Loop S., 713/963-0700, www.druryhotels.com, $89 d), offering a free hot breakfast, evening social hour, a fitness center, indoor/outdoor pool, and whirlpool. Guest rooms feature free Internet access, microwaves, and refrigerators. Similarly priced and amenity packed is the adjacent **La Quinta Inn and Suites** (1625 W. Loop S., 713/355-3440, www.lq.com, $85 d), with a heated pool and spa, a fitness center, free deluxe continental breakfast buffet, and rooms with free Internet access.

$100-150
For a modest increase in price, consider the impressive **Hilton Post Oak** (2001 Post Oak Blvd., 713/961-9300, www.hilton.com, $129 d). Each room includes a balcony offering impressive skyline views, as well as Wi-Fi access, minibars, and refrigerators. The hotel also offers complimentary shuttle service to destinations within a three-mile radius. Another option favored by many Galleria shoppers is the **JW Marriot on Westheimer** (5150 Westheimer Rd., 713/961-1500, www.marriott.com, $149 d), a stately 23-floor hotel featuring wireless Internet access, a fitness center, indoor and outdoor pools, and a whirlpool.

$150-200
It's a bit more expensive, but you'll certainly enjoy a unique and memorable experience at **❰ Hotel Derek** (2525 W. Loop S., 866/292-4100, www.hotelderek.com, $150 d). This independent option is contemporary and sophisticated, with consistently reliable service. Hotel Derek's highlights include an outstanding pool with gushing waterfall, day-spa treatments, and the Derek Mobile, a black stretch SUV providing free transportation to the Galleria's nearby shopping locales (or business meetings). Rooms feature free Wi-Fi access, minibars, CD players with extensive libraries, bathrobes, and beds with goose-down duvets. The hotel's restaurant, Bistro Moderne, is a destination itself, with remarkable French cuisine.

Galleria visitors also enjoy setting up shop at **Embassy Suites** (2911 Sage Rd., 713/626-5444, www.embassysuites.com, $169 d). Guests are immediately greeted by an almost-overwhelming lobby featuring a lofty atrium with a jungle-themed waterway containing swans. Hotel amenities include an indoor pool and whirlpool, a large fitness center, a free cooked-to-order breakfast, and an evening social reception. Rooms offer a private bedroom and separate living area with a sofa bed, minibar, refrigerator, microwave, and Internet access.

The Galleria draws some big spenders, and the surrounding area accommodates them with several pricey lodging options. Among them are **Doubletree Guest Suites** (5353 Westheimer Rd., 713/961-9000, www.doubletree.com, $159 d). In addition to its ideal location, the hotel offers spacious one- and two-bedroom suites with wireless Internet access, a fancy fitness center, and a large outdoor pool area with sundeck and whirlpool.

$200-250
If shopping is a priority, consider staying in a hotel connected to the country's fourth-largest mall. The **Westin Galleria Houston** (5060 W. Alabama St., 713/960-8100, www.starwood-hotels.com, $200 d) is in a prime location, allowing guests to walk straight from the hotel to the massive attached shopping center. After a full day of browsing stores (or even leaving the hotel to explore nearby restaurants, taverns, and cultural attractions), you can unwind in a

spacious room with Internet access (for a fee) and high-quality bedding. Another worthy option is **Staybridge Suites Houston Galleria Area** (5160 Hidalgo St., 800/465-4329, www.ichotelsgroup.com, $209 d), featuring full kitchens, separate sitting and work areas, free Internet access and printing capacities, a fitness center, and outdoor pool.

Kirby District-Rice Village

Downtown is pretty quiet most nights, but Rice Village is usually hoppin'. Visitors often opt to stay here for the abundant nearby nightlife and cultural attractions. One of the best deals in the area is the **Courtyard Houston West University** (2929 Westpark Dr., 713/661-5669, www.marriott.com, $119 d), offering an outdoor pool/whirlpool, exercise room, book-filled library, and free Internet access. Similarly priced yet slightly more upscale is the **Renaissance Greenway Plaza** (6 Greenway Plaza E., 713/629-1200, www.marriott.com, $129 d), featuring spacious rooms with walk-in closets, luxury bedding, Internet access, a fitness center, and outdoor pool.

Another worthy option is the **Hilton Houston Plaza** (6633 Travis St., 713/313-4000, www.hilton.com, $139 d). The Hilton includes large suites, minibars, Internet access, a fitness facility, heated swimming pool, and free transportation within a three-mile radius of the hotel.

The lodging jewel of the city's Museum District crown is **Hotel ZaZa** (5701 Main St., 713/526-1991, www.hotelzaza.com, rooms start at $179). Billed as an "urban resort with a mix of glamour and warmth, high style, and creature comforts," the ZaZa is in a league of its own. Amenities include a poolside retreat and outdoor bar with private cabanas, the luxurious ZaSpa and fitness center, nightly turndown service, cordless phones, free Wi-Fi service, ZaZa guest robes, fancy linens, refrigerators, and an in-room "grab and go gourmet refreshment bar."

Camping

Houston's best camping is about 30 miles southwest of the city at **Brazos Bend State Park** (21901 FM 762, 979/553-5102, www.tpwd.state.tx.us, $4 daily per person 13 and older). Covering roughly 5,000 acres, this popular state park offers hiking, biking, equestrian trails, and fishing on six easily accessible lakes. However, visitors are cautioned about alligators (seriously), which are numerous in some areas of the park. Facilities include restrooms with showers, campsites with water and electricity, screened shelters, primitive equestrian campsites, and a dining hall. Many visitors make Brazos Bend a weekend destination due to its abundant activities, including free interpretive programs and hikes. A nature center with informative displays contains a "hands-on" alligator discovery area, a model of the park, a freshwater aquarium, live native snake species, and the George Observatory (open Saturday 3–10 P.M.).

Closer to town is the unremarkable yet convenient **Alexander Deussen County Park** (12303 Sonnier St., 713/440-1587, call for reservation information). Named after a respected Houston geologist, Deussen Park offers basic camping services, including site pads, fire pits, picnic areas, and restrooms. Pets are allowed, but they must be kept on a leash.

FOOD

Houston has more than 8,000 restaurants (that's not a misprint). People here love eating out, and the array of options is overwhelming, from lowly fast food to lofty haute cuisine. Visitors and residents benefit from the city's enormous international population, offering authentic fare from all corners of the globe, including specific regional styles not found in most midsize cities. This being Texas, the options also include a fair number of home-grown varieties, including some of the state's finest barbecue, Tex-Mex, and good ol' fashioned down-home Southern cookin'.

Downtown
STEAK

A steak house doesn't have to be stodgy. The scene is certainly more swank at **Strip House**

(1200 McKinney St., 713/659-6000, www. striphouse.com/houston, $11–42). The name references the venue's red meat and red decor, a nod to the burlesque theme, but the food is the restaurant's main hook, with sumptuous steaks taking center stage. Featured cuts include the double-cut strip, filet mignon, and porterhouse. The meat is perfectly prepared and the sides (they cost extra but are well worth it) are ideal accompaniments, including the popular goose-fat potatoes, truffled cream spinach, and roasted wild mushrooms.

Another well-heeled yet nontraditionally bedecked downtown steak house is **Vic & Anthony's** (1510 Texas St., 713/228-1111, www.vicandanthonys.com, $15–40). Chic, minimalist, and tightly packed, Vic & Anthony's wisely sticks with the basics—a simple menu offers high-quality cuts of meat and a few seafood and chicken options. The salads and appetizers here are outstanding (the pear salad and oysters, in particular), and the wine selection is impressive, if a bit pricey. The steaks are enormous, and the bone-in rib eye is considered among the best in town.

CAJUN

Houston is one of the few places in the country that serves authentic Cajun cuisine. The Bayou City has direct access to the seafood, sauces, spices, and swamps—the style's integral ingredients. It doesn't get much better than the legendary New Orleans family establishment **Brennan's** (3300 Smith St., 713/522-9712, www.brennanshouston.com, $10–36). Located in a historic brick mansion, Brennan's offers classic Louisiana flavors such as étouffée, lump crab cakes, and pecan-crusted amberjack. The breakfasts at Brennan's are legendary, and the eggs and delectable sauces taste even better paired with live jazz music during the weekend New Orleans Jazz Brunch. Less formal is the popular downtown lunch chain **Treebeard's** (several locations, including 315 Travis St., 713/228-2622, www.treebeards. com, $6–13, weekdays 11 A.M.–2 P.M.). All the Creole classics are here—shrimp étouffée, jambalaya, gumbo, and a hearty dose of red

beans and rice. Be sure to order a side of jalapeño corn bread, and save room for the bread pudding with whiskey sauce. The only drawback: Treebeard's isn't open on weekends or for dinner.

Uptown
LEBANESE

One of the benefits of being in a cosmopolitan environment is the abundance of international cuisine in various formats. Houston's Uptown area contains several noteworthy informal lunch venues, and the best among them serve savory Lebanese food. One of the favorites is **Mary'z Lebanese Cuisine** (5825 Richmond Ave., 832/251-1955, www.maryzcuisine.com, $6–15). It's a tiny place, but the tastes are huge, especially in fresh-made favorites like kabobs, falafel, shawarma, and baba ghanoush. Complement your meal with a Lebanese beer like Almazo. At night, Mary'z becomes a hot spot for young adults who toke on hookahs and exchange phone numbers. A larger and more traditional option is **Café Lili Lebanese Grill** (5757 Westheimer Rd., 713/952-6969, www. cafelili.com, $7–16). This mom-and-pop establishment is a no-frills operation that focuses on the most important things: exemplary food and service. Start off with spinach pie, hummus, or tabouleh, and proceed to the kafta kabobs or lamb dishes. Top it all off with their signature strong coffee.

CONTINENTAL

One of the most popular restaurants in the food-filled Uptown area is **DaMarco** (1520 Westheimer Rd., 713/807-8857, www.damarcohouston.com, $11–32). Known for its splashy colors and equally bold food, DaMarco's is the showcase of renowned Italian-born chef Marco Wiles. Diners are faced with the daunting task of choosing from Tuscan- to Texas-inspired dishes, including savory Chianti-braised pork ribs, sea bass with grilled grapefruit, flavorful lamb chops, and roasted Texas quail. Locals also can't get enough of the classy **RDG+Bar Annie** (1728 Post Oak Blvd., 713/840-1111, www.rdgbarannie.com, $12–39). Elegance exudes from the decor and the dishes, starting with tantalizing appetizers such as goat cheese crepes and continuing with entrées like the cinnamon-roasted pheasant and cocoa-roasted chicken. Haute Texas cuisine is well represented in the cilantro-enhanced mussel soup and barbecued sweet potatoes. Take note: Many locals still refer to this locale as Café Annie, its previous name. Reservations are highly recommended.

Montrose and Kirby Area
MEXICAN

A visit to the Galleria is incomplete without a meal at the tremendous (C **Hugo's** (1600 Westheimer Rd, 713/524-7744, www.hugos-restaurant.net, $12–33). This open-air, chic hacienda serves trendy Mexican dishes sizzling with *sabor* (flavor). Start with Hugo's signature velvety margarita, paired with a tantalizing appetizer, such as the squash-blossom quesadillas or one of four varieties of ceviche. Entrées range from savory pork carnitas to tender snapper Veracruzana. Desserts are legendary at Hugo's, especially the options containing freshly roasted and ground cocoa beans (flan, Mexican hot chocolate).

Another trendy spot with fantastic food is **Armando's** (2630 Westheimer Rd., 713/520-1738, $10–22). Hipsters and regulars arrive early for the potent happy hour margaritas and stick around for the classic Tex-Mex dishes with a twist. Enchiladas are filled with crab and vegetables, and beef dishes are prepared with savory sauces. Unfortunately, the beans are bland, but Armando's is known around town for its tasty *sopapillas* (pillowy pastries topped with honey and powdered sugar).

More traditional in approach yet equally commendable in taste is **Molina's** (7901 Westheimer Rd., 713/782-0861, www.molinasrestaurants.com, $8–15). A Houston institution for nearly seven decades, Molina's is the ultimate destination for old-school Tex-Mex. The signature Mexico City Dinner captures it all: chili con queso, tamale, tostada, taco, and enchilada with requisite rice and beans. Similar in approach and quality is **El Patio**

Mexican Restaurant (6444 Westheimer Rd., 713/780-0410, www.elpatio.com, $8–18). El Patio is also known for its rollicking bar Club No Minors, named for the legal notice posted on the door. The other main draw here is the fajita plate, a steaming dish of savory beef and chicken accompanied by cheddar cheese and piquant pico de gallo. The chicken enchiladas and chiles rellenos are also popular menu items.

AMERICAN

Houstonians go berserk over **Backstreet Café** (1103 S. Shepherd Dr., 713/521-2239, www.backstreetcafe.net, $10–26). This wildly popular two-story New American venue is revered for its crafty chef (Hugo Ortega of Hugo's), who specializes in quality comfort food. Backstreet is particularly known for its "crusted" dishes, including mustard-crusted salmon and sesame-crusted shrimp. The most popular entrée is the meat loaf tower, an aptly named stack of seasoned meat, garlic mashed potatoes, sautéed spinach, and mushroom gravy. Backstreet breakfasts are also legendary, as is the Sunday jazz brunch (11 A.M.–3 P.M.).

Also popular with the locals is (C **Benjy's** (2424 Dunstan Rd., 713/522-7602, www.benjys.com, $11–28), a contemporary venue with outstanding food and service. Things change often here, from the artwork to the menu, keeping things fresh for the regulars and kitchen staff. Seafood is the specialty (smoked salmon, seasoned shrimp), but Benjy's also serves comfort food with modern flair, including distinctive sandwiches and entrées such as the pecan- and pistachio-crusted chicken with mixed potato gratin. Locals flock to Benjy's for brunch, and their Bloody Marys are some of the best in the city (they use wasabi instead of regular horseradish).

Another trendy and tasty option is **Mockingbird Bistro** (1985 Welch St., 713/533-0200, www.mockingbirdbistro.com, $11–32), nestled in a dark yet comfy historic building in a well-heeled neighborhood. Diners can elect to go small (the "bar bites" offer mini portions of ribs, risotto, and mussels) or large (the entrées are generously sized). Popular menu items include the onion soup, seared tuna steak, pork chop, and steak au poivre. Save room for the chocolate-themed desserts.

LUNCH

Most restaurants in this traditionally trendy part of town have impressive lunch menus, but a few places are noteworthy for their vibrant scenes. Among them is **Goode Co. Barbeque** (5109 Kirby Dr., 713/522-2530, www.goodecompany.com, $9–19), a funky spot that's always packed with students, young professionals, and working-class carnivores. Goode's specializes in classic 'cue—sausage, ribs, chicken, and the signature tender and juicy brisket—all topped with a succulent and smoky sauce. The side items are better than average, including a sweet coleslaw and bitey jalapeño corn bread.

On the opposite end of the cultural and social spectrum is the sleek **Ra Sushi** (3908 Westheimer Rd., 713/621-5800, www.rasushi.com, $5–17). Drawing a young crowd of busy singles, Ra is known for its stylish social scene as much as its hip sushi rolls. Popular items include the spicy lobster roll, scallop dynamite, and Viva Las Vegas roll with light tempura, crab, tuna, and lotus root. Consider ordering one of the seaweed salads or a more substantial item from the Pacific Rim–themed full menu. Stick around for the happy hour scene at Ra's Flying Fish Lounge.

Outlying Areas
AMERICAN

Burger fans take note: **Becks Prime** (2615 Augusta Dr., 713/266-9901, www.becksprime.com, $7–18) is just about as good as it gets. Upscale burgers with top-quality meat and sensational seasonings are typically found only in fancier restaurants with tablecloths and wine menus. Not here. The fast-food vibe tricks your senses with lowered expectations, but the massive burger you hold in your hands has all the makings of a classic: thick, juicy high-quality ground beef and fresh toppings on a soft, sweet bun. You'll never want to bite into a chain-store burger again. Becks also serves equally tantalizing steaks (and milk shakes). Becks operates several downtown-area restaurants, but the Augusta Drive location has especially pleasant scenery, thanks to several colossal outstretched oak trees on the grounds.

Meat is also the main attraction at **Pizzitola's Bar-B-Cue** (1703 Shepherd Dr., 713/227-2283, $9–18), a legendary barbecue joint with a forgettable exterior and name. This old-fashioned locale has been around since the 1930s, when it was known as Shepherd Drive Barbecue, and the decades of hickory-smoked goodness have lingered ever since. Tender ribs and brisket are the big draw here, and the spicy sauce subtly enhances both. Another bonus: Warm towels are available for post-eating sauce removal. Be sure to save room (or place a takeout order) for the amazing desserts, particularly the coconut pineapple cake and banana pudding.

Those craving fresh seafood won't regret the 30-mile drive to **TopWater Grill** (815 Ave. O in the small town of San Leon, 281/339-1232, www.topwatergrill.com, $8–24). Nestled in an unassuming building on the bay, Top Water is high on the list of fishermen's favorites, thanks to the quality fresh catches and understated yet effective seasoning and preparation. Start with the plump and flavorful peel-and-eat shrimp (or fried, or grilled), and complete your feast with the snapper, swordfish, or redfish. It's advisable to fill up on the fresh seafood only and not waste valuable stomach space with the iceberg lettuce salad or fried side items (hush puppies and fries).

CHINESE

Houston has a sizable Chinese population, and the plethora of restaurants provide an impressive representation of the various styles of national cuisine. Topping most foodies' lists is **Fung's Kitchen** (7320 Southwest Frwy., 713/779-2288, www.fungskitchen.com, $10–36), a haven for fresh seafood. This is fancy stuff, so don't be surprised by the somewhat lofty yet completely worthwhile prices. Many of the seafood items are still swimming in tanks when you order them, including the soon-to-be lightly seasoned and heavily flavorful lobster, crab, and cod. With more than 400 items to choose from, the menu is somewhat overwhelming but ultimately tantalizing in its impressive array of items. Dim sum fans will be pleasantly surprised and rewarded with the vast number of quality options.

Less distinguished yet more appealing to the masses is **Yao Restaurant & Bar** (9755 Westheimer Rd., 832/251-2588, www.yaorestaurant.com, $10–29), run by the parents of Houston Rockets basketball star Yao Ming. This upscale establishment focuses on the classics—Peking duck, Szechuan prawn, and mu shu pork—in a modern Asian setting with several large-screen televisions broadcasting sporting events. The food isn't very adventurous, but it's high-quality stuff. In fact, it may be one of the best meals you'll experience while watching a game on TV.

An interesting place to go for dim sum—the traditional Chinese custom of ordering individual items from roving carts—is **Kim Son** (2001 Jefferson St., 281/222-2461, www.kimson.com, $10–30). Though it's technically a Vietnamese restaurant, the dim-sum custom, like many families in Houston, crosses cultures. If you've never experienced this unique approach to enjoying a meal, this is the place to do it: Pan-fried and steamed seafood dumplings, sticky rice, seaweed-wrapped shrimp, and mushroom-capped meatballs are just a few of the dozens of enticing items awaiting your selection at Kim Son.

MEXICAN

Not too far away from downtown is the fantastic **Pico's** (5941 Bellaire Blvd., 713/662-8383, www.picos.net, $9–23). Billing itself as "Mex-Mex," Pico's offers interior Mexican food with some flair. Specialties include the bacon-wrapped shrimp with poblano pepper stuffing, pollo pibil (marinated chicken wrapped in banana leaves), and smooth yet spicy mole sauces. Things get a bit festive here, especially on weekends, when diners enjoy margaritas and mariachis on the palapa-covered patio.

For a more traditional Tex-Mex experience, head to **Doneraki Restaurant** (300 Gulfgate Mall, 713/645-6400, www.doneraki.com, $9–20), a classic joint complete with a massive Diego Rivera mural. The taste is huge here, too, especially in the perfectly seasoned meat dishes. Try the beef fajitas and chicken enchiladas, and appreciate the fact that the chips, salsa, and bowl-scraping chili con queso are free at lunch.

For some of the best Mexican home-style cooking in Houston, visit **Otilla's Mexican Restaurant** (7710 Long Point Rd., 713/681-7203, www.otilias.com, $8–19, closed Mon.). What Otilla's lacks in atmosphere (it's housed in a former fast-food drive-in) it makes up for in spectacular-tasting food. Like most interior-leaning locales, the velvety mole sauce is outstanding here, but it's the á la carte items that make a visit to Otilla's imminently worthwhile. Load up on gorditas, chiles rellenos, cochinita pibil, and the tres leches cake for an unforgettable experience in a forgettable building.

VEGETARIAN

Houston is generally more about beef than veggies, but there are a few safe havens for vegetarians. The most acclaimed spot, **Baba Yega** (2607 Grant St., 713/522-0042, www.babayega.com, $8–21), is not exclusively vegetarian, but the meat-free dishes are considered some of the city's finest. The salads, pasta, and sandwiches here are legendary, including the tasty veggie club (turkey, fake bacon, and provolone) and Tuesday Italian Special (pasta and wine combo). The owner's adjacent herb shop is the source for many of Baba Yega's fresh and flavorful seasonings.

Also not technically a full vegetarian restaurant, the popular **Hobbit Cafe** (2243 Richmond Ave., 713/526-5460, www.myhobbitcafe.com, $7–17) serves earthy fare in a forestlike setting surrounded by a white picket fence. Soups and salads are the specialty here, including the ambrosial fruit salad and tropical chicken salad, and the veggie burgers are as charming as the mystical decor. The Hobbit Cafe also has a well-deserved reputation for serving delicious desserts, including moist carrot cake and tangy Key lime pie.

For a cheap and flavorful veggie meal, drop by the magnificent **Shri Balaji Bhavan** (5655 Hillcroft Dr., 713/783-1126, $4–12). This is hot stuff, but for the price—most entrées average around $5—you can't go wrong. The cuisine is primarily South Indian, including spicy yet well-balanced dishes such as rasam soup, chole, and dal.

INFORMATION AND SERVICES

For detailed information about specific companies and service agencies offering Houston visitor information, see the *Information and Services* at the beginning of this chapter. Meanwhile, here's a quick overview: The **Greater Houston Convention and Visitors Bureau** (901 Bagby St., Suite 100, 713/437-5200, www.visithoustontexas.com, daily 9 A.M.–4 P.M.) can handle most visitor needs. The CVB operates brochure- and map-filled offices at City Hall (Bagby Street location), Katy Mills Mall (just off I-10 about 15 miles west of town), and the Bay Area Houston Visitors Center (off Highway 45 about 15 miles southeast of town).

To find out what's going on in the city and beyond, pick up a copy of the respected **Houston Chronicle** (www.chron.com), the city's only metro daily. The *Chronicle* provides detailed coverage of city and state news, as well as detailed listings of restaurants and entertainment venues. For information about local politics and arts happenings, pick up a free copy of the **Houston Press** (www.houstonpress.com) at businesses and bus stations across town.

GETTING THERE AND AROUND

Houston's major airport is **George Bush Intercontinental Airport** (2800 N. Terminal Rd., 281/230-3100, www.fly2houston.com), located just north of town. The city's old airport, **William P. Hobby Airport** (8183 Airport Blvd., 713/640-3000, www.fly2houston.com), is now the major hub for Southwest Airlines.

SuperShuttle (281/230-7275, www.supershuttle.com) provides shuttle service between both airports and downtown-area hotels. To arrange for cab pick-up service from within the city, contact the following local companies: **Liberty Cab Company** (281/540-8294), **Square Deal Cab Co.** (713/444-4444), **Lonestar Cab** (713/794-0000), and **United Cab Co.** (713/699-0000). To rent a car from the airport, contact the **Consolidated Rental Car Facility** (281/233-3000, www.iahrac.com). All the major rental car companies are accessible, and they share a shuttle system.

To reach the city by bus, leave the driving to **Houston Greyhound** (2121 Main St., 713/759-6565 or 800/231-2222, www.greyhound.com). Trains arrive and depart at the Houston Amtrak station (902 Washington Ave., 713/224-1577 or 800/872-7245, www.amtrak.com) via Amtrak's Sunset Limited line.

Houston's public transportation system, the Metro, aka the **Metropolitan Transit Authority of Harris County** (713/635-4000, www.ridemetro.org), offers local and commuter bus service. Tickets are available in vending machines located at each station.

BEAUMONT AND VICINITY

Beaumont (population 109,856) isn't your average Texas midsize city. It's more connected to the eastern United States than other Southern communities, it's a working-class union town (due to the propensity of oil riggers), and it has a denser historic downtown than its wide-open West Texas brethren. Its proximity to New Orleans and the Gulf Coast along with its two nearby sister cities of Port Arthur and Orange have earned the area the nickname "the Cajun Triangle."

The city's (and state's and country's) fate was forever changed on the morning of January 10, 1901, when the Lucas Gusher erupted from the Spindletop oilfield. Tens of thousands of people flocked to Beaumont to capitalize on the oil boom and, in the process, built an impressive collection of churches, civic buildings, and residences. The impact on Beaumont resulted in a true American melting pot, with Italian and Jewish influences combined with Cajun and African-American inspirations. The city's architectural treasures remain an integral part of downtown's distinctive historical charm.

Although the corporate oil scene would eventually move to nearby Houston (about 90 miles to the southwest), Beaumont's petroleum-related legacy remains its true identity. In 1901, the first year of the boom, three major companies formed—the Gulf Oil Corporation, Humble (later Exxon), and the Texas Company (later Texaco). One year later, more than 500 Texas corporations were doing business in Beaumont.

However, the boom soon went bust, as Spindletop quickly fell victim to an overabundance of wells. Two decades later, new advancements in the oil industry allowed riggers to dig wells deeper, resulting in another Spindletop boom. In 1927, the oilfield yielded its all-time annual high of 21 million barrels.

The Beaumont area never experienced another major surge, but the city had landed on the map, with corporations and families from across the country relocating to the region. During World War II the city prospered as a shipbuilding center, and the petrochemical industry continued to sustain the economy for decades to come.

Meanwhile, the nearby coastal communities of Port Arthur and Orange benefited from Beaumont's corporate and cultural activity. Although the oil money never made the Golden Triangle as prosperous as its name implies, the region benefited by opening several art museums, forging a soulful music identity, and capitalizing on its Cajun culture by developing fabulous food establishments.

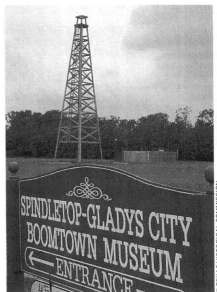

© TEXAS HISTORICAL COMMISSION

the Spindletop-Gladys City Boomtown Museum

offers a self-guided tour of 15 clapboard building replicas from the oil-boom era, including a general store, saloon, post office, stable, and blacksmith shop. The buildings and associated photos and interpretative panels tell the story of the massive and unprecedented boomtown saga, where Beaumont transformed from a village of several hundred to a city of nearly 30,000 in a matter of weeks. The museum also features wooden oil derricks of the era, including a life-size water-spewing gusher that keeps families entertained and refreshed during the hot summer months.

◖ Spindletop-Gladys City Boomtown Museum

To get a true sense of the craziness that befell Beaumont upon the discovery of the Spindletop oilfield, visit the intriguing Spindletop-Gladys City Boomtown Museum (5550 University Dr., 409/835-0823, www.spindletop.org, Tues.– Sat. 10 A.M.–5 P.M., Sun. 1–5 P.M., $3 adults, $2 seniors, $1 children). Located near the site of the famous Lucas gusher, the museum

McFaddin-Ward House

One of the city's top tourist destinations is the remarkable 1906 McFaddin-Ward House (1906 Calder Ave., 409/832-2134, www.mcfaddin-ward.org, Tues.–Sat. 10 A.M.–3 P.M., Sun. 1–3 P.M., closed at lunch, $3 guided tours, $1 self-guided tour; reservations recommended). This impressive neoclassical, Beaux-Arts–style mansion features beautiful decorative exterior detailing and opulent interior furnishings reflecting the lifestyle of William McFaddin, a member of one of Texas's oldest and wealthiest families. McFaddin was a Texas Army veteran who created a cattle and oil empire from the land he received for his military service. The guided tours of his family's fabulous home and adjacent carriage house provide anecdotal and architectural background information along with up-close views of furniture, artwork, and mementos showcasing this prominent Texas family.

Texas Energy Museum

Somewhat surprisingly, Beaumont boasts nearly 20 museums. Among the best is the downtown Texas Energy Museum (600 Main St., 409/833-5100, www.texasenergymuseum. org, Tues.–Sat. 9 A.M.–5 P.M., Sun. 1–5 P.M., $2 adults, $1 seniors and children ages 6–12). This spacious two-story facility features a fascinating collection of exhibits dedicated to, appropriately enough, oil-based energy sources. Interactive displays highlight the history of oil as a versatile resource and provide vital information about the global significance of this local commodity. Though the name is somewhat misleading—there aren't any power plants or light bulbs here—the museum succeeds in educating visitors about the remarkable history and relevance of the petrochemical industry.

Fire Museum of Texas

The nearby Fire Museum of Texas (400 Walnut St., 409/880-3927, www.firemuseumoftexas. org, Mon.–Fri. 8 A.M.–4:30 P.M., free admission) is another unexpected gem. The small museum, housed in the 1927 Beaumont Fire Department Headquarters Station, is practically dwarfed by the massive black-and-white-spotted "world's largest fire hydrant" in front of the building. Now considered the third largest in the world, this 24-foot-tall hydrant was donated to the museum by Disney Studios in conjunction with the release of the animated movie *101 Dalmatians*. Inside, the facility showcases the importance of firefighters in Texas and across the country through vintage

the 24-foot tall fire hydrant at the Fire Museum of Texas

© TEXAS HISTORICAL COMMISSION

fire engines and equipment, educational exhibits, and the Texas Firefighter Memorial.

Babe Didrickson Zaharias Museum

Babe who? You'll be telling everyone about her after experiencing the captivating Babe Didrickson Zaharias Museum (1750 I-10 E., 409/833-4622, www.babedidriksonzaharias. org, daily 9 A.M.–5 P.M., free admission). Port Arthur native Zaharias was a pioneer in women's sports who was voted the world's greatest woman athlete of the first half of the 20th century in a poll conducted by the Associated Press. Nicknamed "Babe" after swatting five home runs in one baseball game, Zaharias was an accomplished Olympic athlete, tennis player, basketball player, diver, bowler, and, most notably, golfer. She won every major professional golf championship at least once and is credited with single-handedly popularizing women's golf. The museum features trophies, golf clubs, photos, newspaper clippings, Olympic medals, and films representing her fascinating and enormously successful athletic career.

Accommodations

For a small city, Beaumont is surprisingly lacking in recommendable rooms at discounted rates as well as downtown hotels within walking distance of the city's many museums and cultural attractions. Regardless, one of the better deals in town is **La Quinta Midtown** (220 I-10 N., 409/838-9991, www.lq.com, $69 d), located about five minutes from the city center on busy I-10. La Quinta offers a free continental breakfast, free Internet access, and an outdoor pool.

A popular and reliable option is **Sleep Inn & Suites** (2030 N. 11th St., 409/892-6700, www.choicehotels.com, $79 d), featuring free wireless Internet access, a free deluxe continental breakfast, fitness center, and an outdoor pool.

The best bang for the buck is **◖ Holiday Inn Beaumont-Plaza** (3950 I-10 S., 409/842-5995 or 800/465-4329, www.holidayinn.com,

$89 d). An enormous three-story cascading waterfall greets guests as they enter the spacious garden atrium, and the renovated rooms provide clean and comfortable accommodations. The Plaza location (not to be confused with Holiday Inn Midtown) features free Wi-Fi service, an indoor pool and whirlpool, full-feature fitness center, and free meals for kids 12 and under.

Representing the upper tier of Beaumont's lodging options is the regional chain **MCM Elegante** (2355 I-10 S., 409/842-3600, www.mcmelegantebeaumont.com, $139 d). The hotel features a tropical outdoor pool, a fancy fitness center, free Wi-Fi access, refrigerators, and microwaves.

Food

CROCKETT STREET DISTRICT

It's only one city block, but the historic Crockett Street District is a fun little stretch of downtown that gives Beaumont an extra dash of flavor. The area was once the center of illicit activity, with bordellos and bars

the Crockett Street entertainment district

keeping roughnecks and port visitors plenty entertained. These days, most of the establishments are respectable bars and restaurants. If you're only in town one day, go to **Spindletop Steakhouse** (290 Crockett St., 409/833-2433, $10–29). Housed in the city's historic oil exchange building, the restaurant is a worthy representation of Beaumont, with photos, artifacts, and decor harkening back to the boomtown days. The real draw, however, is the food—a hearty sampling of local favorites, from thick, flavorful steaks to perfectly prepared pasta to thick, spicy gumbo. A word of caution: The soft, warm bread served before your meal is so tasty, you'll be tempted to eat the whole loaf before your meal arrives. Enjoy it in moderation.

Just a few doors down is **Rio Rita's Mexican Food & Cantina** (230 Crockett St., 490/833-0750, $8–16). Be sure to request a table on the balcony, a pleasant wrought-iron second-story setting reminiscent of New Orleans. If it's full (which it often is), the backup plan is perfectly acceptable: a table on the pleasant ground-floor patio with fountain. You can't go wrong with the food here, either. Rio Rita's specializes in classic Tex-Mex, with sizzling fajitas, stuffed enchiladas, and seasoned nachos among the locals' favorites. Enhance your experience with a smooth and potent house margarita.

CAJUN AND SEAFOOD

Beaumont is one of the best places in Texas to get authentic Cajun food, and the city's proximity to the Gulf means the seafood is always immensely fresh and flavorful. A favorite among locals is the no-frills **Sartin's West** (6680 Calder Ave., 409/861-3474, closed Mon., $9–20). Beaumonters can't get enough of their fantastic barbecued crabs, and for good reason: These tasty morsels are succulent and slightly spicy, an ideal representation of Beaumont's distinctive cuisine. Other popular menu items include the broiled seafood platter and any variety of shrimp (fried, grilled, or peel-and-eat).

Another spot where locals line up is the consistently delectable **Vautrot's Cajun Cuisine** (13350 Hwy. 105, 409/753-2015, www.vautrots.com, $7–18, closed Sun. and Mon.). Start with the tasty crawfish étouffée or jam-packed gumbo, or go crazy and proceed directly to the ridiculously large and immensely flavorful Uncle Emrick's Seafood Sampler, containing the gumbo and étouffée along with fried crawfish, fried catfish, fried shrimp, fried oysters, onion rings or French fries, and a healthy salad.

Floyd's Cajun Seafood (2290 I-10 S., 409/842-0686, www.floydsseafood.com, $8–19) is a small regional chain that's huge on authentic flavor. You'll find all the reliable standards here, from crawfish and shrimp to oysters and catfish.

Information and Services

To get a handle on the layout of the city and where things are in relation to your hotel, contact the friendly folks at the **Beaumont Convention & Visitors Bureau** (505 Willow St., 409/880-3749 or 800/392-4401, www.beaumontcvb.com). Maps, brochures, and staff members are available at the CVB's information centers. The main office, 505 Willow Street, is open Monday–Friday 8 A.M.–5 P.M. The other visitors center is at the Babe Zaharias Museum at 1750 I-10 (exit 854), 409/833-4622, open daily 9 A.M.–5 P.M.

Port Arthur

With three major oil refineries in operation, the coastal city of Port Arthur's (population 55,745) economy remains primarily petro-centered. Named for Arthur Stillwell, a Kansas City businessman who brought the railroad to town, this low-key community has been tied to the shipping industry since a navigable canal was dredged in the early 1900s.

Aside from oil and ocean commerce, Port Arthur is known for churning out music stars (Janis Joplin, the Big Bopper, Johnny Winter, and Tex Ritter are area natives) as well as its Cajun food, fishing, and legendary Mardi Gras celebration, drawing tens of thousands of people each February for the festive atmosphere.

SIGHTS

Get a grasp on the Golden Triangle's illustrious history at the **Museum of the Gulf Coast** (700 Proctor St., 409/982-7000, Mon.–Sat. 9 A.M.–5 P.M., Sun. 1–5 P.M., $4 adults, $3 seniors, $2 students ages 6–18). Located in a large downtown two-story former bank building, the museum covers a lot of ground. From prehistoric items to Texas Revolution artifacts to modern mementos, the Museum of the Gulf Coast offers a comprehensive representation of cultural events in the region. Be sure to check out the replica of Janis Joplin's painted psychedelic Porsche in the museum's music exhibit, where visitors can play songs on a jukebox (for free) and browse among the displays dedicated to the surprising number of musicians from the area, including Joplin, George Jones, the Big Bopper, Tex Ritter, and members of ZZ Top. Nearby, a similarly large (head-scratchingly so) number of sports legends and celebrities are featured in the pop culture exhibit, including Jimmy Johnson, Bum and Wade Phillips, and two *Police Academy* stars (G. W. Bailey and Charles "Bubba" Smith).

The **Sabine Pass Battleground** (6100 Dick Dowling Rd., 512/463-7948, www.visitsabinepassbattleground.com), 12 miles south of town, is worth visiting even if you aren't a history buff. Acquired by the Texas Historical Commission, this 58-acre site tells the story of a fierce Civil War battle where severely outnumbered Confederate troops prevailed over a formidable Union fleet. Interpretive panels and a big bronze statue help portray the conflict, and visitors have access to walking trails and camping facilities overlooking the Sabine Ship Channel.

For a unique experience, drop by the **Buu Mon Buddhist Temple** (2701 Procter St., 409/982-9319, www.buumon.org). Established as the first Buddhist center in Beaumont (an inspiration for the name), the temple is now located in a former Baptist and Vietnamese Catholic church. Where there was once a steeple, a stupa now exists. Instead of a crucifix, a seven-foot-tall gilt bronze Buddha now rests on the altar. The temple's annual spring garden

Buu Mon Buddhist Temple

© TEXAS HISTORICAL COMMISSION

tour attracts hundreds of Texans in search of pleasing colors and smells in the lotus garden. Monks are always on hand to enthusiastically guide visitors through the temple and the garden, and even offer a cup of freshly brewed green tea.

FOOD

Port Arthur is known across Texas for its excellent seafood and Cajun restaurants. One of the best spots in town is the bland-looking yet consistently tasty **Bruce's Seafood Deli** (6801 9th Ave., 409/727-3184, $8–18). You can't go wrong with the basics here—shrimp, crawfish, and catfish. Another favorite Bayou-style eatery is **Larry's French Market and Cajun Cafeteria** (3701 Atlantic Hwy. in nearby Groves, 409/962-3381, www.larrysfrenchmarket.com, $7–19, closed Sun.), offering an ideal all-inclusive combo (the Captain's Platter), featuring fresh and flavorful shrimp, catfish, oysters, barbecue crabs, fried crawfish, seafood gumbo, and Cajun fries. Alternate menu options include the "boiled water critters" (crawfish and crab) served with corn, potatoes, and a dipping sauce, as well as fried critters (alligator, frog legs).

Locals tend to loiter at traditionally minded and decorated **The Schooner** (1507 S. Hwy. 69, 409/722-2323, $8–23). Seafood is the main catch here, ranging from fresh fillets to fried platters. Popular menu items include the broiled fillet of snapper, stuffed crab, and oysters.

Orange

One of Texas's easternmost and oldest cities is Orange (population 18,113), a border town (with Louisiana) named for orange groves along the Sabine River. It never experienced the same gushing levels of successful oil activity as Beaumont and Port Arthur, but it was an important industrial port during the two World Wars, boasting an all-time-high population of 60,000 in the mid-1940s.

Decades earlier, Orange was infamous for its red-light district and outlaw reputation. Its respectability increased when shipbuilding kept the local economy afloat during wartime. Though many residents fled to larger cities in subsequent decades, Orange continues to draw hordes of fishermen and outdoors enthusiasts for its abundant hunting, birding, and fresh- and salt-water fishing.

SIGHTS

You're already in the bayou, so why not *really* get into the bayou? **Adventures 2000-plus Swamp and River Tours** (409/883-0856, www.swampandrivertours.com, several tours offered daily [call for reservations], $25 adults, $20 seniors and students, $15 children 11 and under). Adventures 2000-plus educates locals and visitors about the fascinating biodiversity of the region, so don't look for any high-powered, speedy water vessels here. Instead, the boats are designed for comfort and relative quiet, allowing a better chance of seeing wild alligators, eagles, rare birds, and various swamp plants and creatures. Note: As of early 2011, the company was still operating tours regularly but was in search of new ownership. Check

beforehand regarding a potential change in name, hours of operation, etc.

On the opposite end of the cultural scale is the highbrow **Stark Museum of Art** (712 Green Ave., 409/886-2787, Tues.–Sat. 10 A.M.–5 P.M., free admission). Named for Orange native Henry J. Lutcher Stark, a successful lumber baron and entrepreneur, the museum showcases the family's extensive collection of art related to the American West. Paintings, prints, and sculpture depict the breathtaking landscapes and natural features of the West, along with other artistic mediums such as bronze Remington sculptures, Native American pottery and baskets, and Steuben crystal.

To learn more about the intriguing life of the Stark family, visit the remarkable **W.H. Stark House** (610 W. Main St., 409/883-0871, www.whstarkhouse.org, Tues.–Sat. 10 A.M.–3 P.M., $5 adults, $2 seniors and children ages 10–17). The magnificent 1894 Queen Anne mansion contains 15 rooms of opulent furnishings, artwork, carpet, and silver and porcelain settings. The family's financial success afforded them the rare luxury (in this part of Texas) of purchasing expensive housewares and artwork, including fancy cut glass, imported bronzes, and Asian antiques. The Stark House is listed on the National Register of Historic Places and is designated a Recorded Texas Historic Landmark by the Texas Historical Commission.

FOOD

Like the other apexes of the Golden Triangle, Orange is known for its top-notch Cajun food. Though the options here are slightly more limited, they're still quality locales. Among them is the **Original Cajun Cookery** (2308 Lutcher Dr., 409/670-1000, www.cajuncookeryorange.com, $9–17). The best menu items are the Cajun classics such as blackened catfish, fried alligator, and hearty gumbo. The lunch and dinner buffets are the way to go—sample the dozens of tasty options for a reasonable price.

Another popular option is **Crazy Jose's** (110 Strickland Dr., 409/883-6106, $7–16). As the name implies, Crazy Jose's is an eclectic mix of Mexican, Cajun, and seafood items, providing a welcome mix of tantalizing flavors, from the superb chiles rellenos to the spicy seafood gumbo to the flaky catfish fillets.

If you're more in the mood for turf than surf, belly up to the consistently reliable **J.B.'s BBQ Restaurant** (5750 Old Hwy. 90, 409/886-9823, $7–16, closed Sun. and Mon.). J.B.'s doesn't offer table service (customers place and pick up their orders at the counter), and that's good news—it means less time to wait on the fabulous food. You can't go wrong with any of the classics here. Ribs, brisket, sausage, and chicken are all perfectly smoked and smothered in a sweet and spicy sauce.

Another popular local hangout is **Spanky's Restaurant** (1703 N. 16th St., 409/886-2949, $6–17). Noteworthy menu items include the mega one-pound "Flookburger" and the deep-fried peppers stuffed with crabmeat and cheese.

Piney Woods

The Piney Woods are the natural heart of East Texas. Comprised of several national forests and not much else, most of this vast area remains as it has for centuries, when Native American tribes and pioneers hunted wild game in the dense woods by day and slept under the canopy of pine boughs by night.

The moniker "Piney Woods," a Texas colloquialism, is an endearing term describing this forested region, an image many visitors don't associate with the stereotypical desert landscape of the Lone Star State. Regardless, these aren't dense, lush, groves of evergreens—they're mainly shortleaf and loblolly pines, sprinkled liberally with hardwoods such as oak, elm, ash, and maple. The combination is especially appealing in autumn, when, in another unexpected Texas scene, occasional bursts of changing colors offer a scenic outdoor escape.

There's no shortage of recreational activities in this portion of East Texas, particularly in the national and state forests and parks, which annually draw tens of thousands of campers, bikers, hikers, fishers, and boaters to their natural playscapes. Texans accustomed to their state's hot summers and unpredictable winters will frequent the recreation areas throughout the year, while out-of-staters prefer to enjoy them during the temperate months of spring and late fall.

These wooded areas provided shelter and sustenance for the region's earliest inhabitants, the Native American tribes that were largely displaced by Westward frontier expansion. The legacy of the Caddo Indians is evident in the rich history of Piney Woods communities like Nacogdoches, and the Alabama-Coushatta tribe remains a vital cultural presence on its reservation in the Big Thicket National Preserve.

The forests also had a significant impact on East Texas's economy when the lumber industry became a major contributor to the state's agricultural output in the late 19th and early 20th centuries. Though much of the area was initially overharvested, the industry eventually recovered and remains an essential economical element today. The Piney Woods community of Lufkin contains several cultural attractions related to the area's timber-oriented past.

◖ BIG THICKET NATIONAL PRESERVE

The Big Thicket National Preserve's name is somewhat misleading. Sure, there are areas of dense forest seemingly impenetrable by man or beast. But for the most part, this National Park Service property is merely woodsy, with pines, oaks, and swamplands dominating the landscape. It's what occupies this flora that makes the Big Thicket a national treasure.

Species from the Gulf Coast, Central Plains, and Southeastern forests coexist with critters from the deserts, bayous, woods, and swamps. Birds from all regions of the country that should never be sharing air space pass through the area on migratory routes. There are 85 tree species, nearly 186 kinds of birds, and 50 reptile species, including a small, rarely seen population of alligators. In short, the tremendous variety of habitats coupled with the thicket's geographic location result in a unique destination for nature lovers and wildlife enthusiasts.

A good place to start is the Big Thicket's visitors center located seven miles north of Kountze at the intersection of U.S. Highway 69 and FM 420 (409/951-6725, daily 9 A.M.–5 P.M.). The center provides brochures and maps, and includes a discovery room with interactive and educational exhibits related to the history and scope of the Big Thicket. Visitors can also view a 30-minute orientation film and have access to a NPS nature guide offering a short excursion to several of the ecosystems found in the preserve.

Those planning to stick around awhile can take advantage of the Big Thicket's many recreational opportunities, including hiking, with eight trails offering more than 45 miles of mild terrain through the muggy forest.

Bikers should head to the preserve's Big Sandy Creek Unit. One of the most popular activities at Big Thicket is bird-watching, and the Big Thicket Loop offers ideal opportunities. Bird migrations peak between March and May, and some of the most sought-after species include the brown leaded nuthatch, the red cockaded woodpecker, and the Bachman's sparrow. Camping is also available, but only at primitive sites (no hookups). Campers must have a valid Backcountry Use Permit, available at the visitors center or headquarters offices.

The preserve is also known for its water-based activities, particularly fishing, popular along the Neches River, Village Creek, and Pine Island Bayou. Preserve rangers require fishers to have a valid State of Texas fishing license. The Big Thicket also contains two major canoe trails, the scenic Neches River and naturally rustic Pine Island Bayou. Find out about other canoeing, kayaking, and boating opportunities throughout the preserve by checking with the visitors center for maps.

The Big Thicket does not charge fees for

LOGGING TIME WITH THE COMPANY

From the 1880s until the 1920s, East Texas's Piney Woods became a lot less piney. And woodsy. During these four decades, the "lumber bonanza" resulted in 18 million acres worth of timber being cut.

Lumber production started out with small owner-operated sawmills and eventually evolved into sophisticated operations that dominated the East Texas economy in the early 1900s. These corporations built their own railroads into the forests and connected their isolated sawmills with major cities and shipping points for their wood products.

One of the more fascinating aspects of this era was the establishment of lumber "company towns." The men who worked in the sawmills and on the cutting crews were encouraged to remain with a company for the long haul, and one of the main incentives was the promise of caring for their wives and children.

The companies would choose a location on a rail line and construct a makeshift town, complete with all the basic necessities, including homes, schools, churches, stores, and hospitals. The workers were often paid with credits they could use for food, merchandise, and services in the company town facilities.

Sometimes, the towns would pick up and move along with the ever-changing frontier of virgin forest. Homes located in rail cars allowed for easy mobility, leaving behind a ghost town of clapboard buildings and dirt roads.

By the 1920s, the depletion of the East Texas timber resources combined with the effect of the Great Depression caused the decline of the lumber bonanza. Some of the companies went into bankruptcy, while several of the larger timber corporations moved to the fertile forests of the Pacific Northwest.

park entrance, activities (aside from fishing and camping permits), education programs, or hunting permits. Naturalist activities are available with reservations, or on selected weekends. Call 409/951-6725 or visit www. nps.gov/bith to learn more about the park and its activities or to find out more about making reservations.

NATIONAL FORESTS

Nearly 750,000 acres of East Texas pine forests remain standing as a result of the involvement of the federal government. The trees were mostly clear-cut during the zealous timber harvesting of the early 1900s, but the U.S. Forest Service eventually became involved as an "administrator" of the vast woodlands, allowing them to be responsibly maintained through professional oversight of harvesting and replenishing.

The four national forests of East Texas are ideal destinations for a natural weekend getaway. Campers will want to pack more than hiking boots and mountain bikes—these

woods are filled with rivers and lakes ideal for canoeing and fishing. Many nearby communities have small shops offering boat rental, fishing supplies, and fishing licenses to address most weekenders' recreational needs.

Angelina National Forest

Located just east of Lufkin, the 153,179-acre Angelina National Forest is one of the most popular East Texas forests for fishing and boating excursions. Angelina completely encapsulates most of the massive Sam Rayburn Reservoir, an 114,500-acre lake on the Angelina River formed when the Sam Rayburn Dam was constructed in the early 1960s.

The forest itself is like most of its East Texas brethren, with gently rolling landscapes covered mostly with shortleaf and loblolly pine, hardwoods, and a swath of longleaf pine in the southern portion. When it was acquired by the federal government in 1935, Angelina was in pretty bad shape—most of the property had been forested and left without adequate protection. The Texas Forest Service's fire prevention

© TEXAS HISTORICAL COMMISSION

ruins of the Aldridge Sawmill in Angelina National Forest

efforts resulted in much of the land "seeding in" naturally, a practice that continues to this day.

Though Angelina is focused primarily on water-based activities, there are several hiking trails available, including access to the historic **Aldridge Sawmill**, where huge concrete structures remain as reminders of the region's timber-industry heritage. To get there, take the 5.5-mile Sawmill Hiking Trail, which follows an old tramway used in the early 1900s to haul logs to the sawmills.

The park's two main recreation areas, Caney Creek and Sandy Creek, offer camping, boating, and fishing on or near the shores of Sam Rayburn Reservoir. Camping and fishing are also popular at Bouton Lake Recreation Area and Boykin Springs Recreation Area, including historic structures built by the Civilian Conservation Corps and offering camping, swimming, fishing, and canoeing.

The Sam Rayburn Reservoir is a popular destination for anglers, who return regularly for the lake's abundant largemouth bass, crappie, and catfish. Recreational boating is also a major activity, with water-skiers, sailboats, and personal watercraft dotting the water's surface.

Visitors also flock to Angelina to view the hundreds of wildlife species, including deer, wild turkey, woodcock, quail, and the year-round resident population of wood ducks. During the winter, bald eagles occupy the area surrounding the reservoir, and the forest is also home to the endangered red-cockaded woodpecker, a small black-and-white bird that visitors often make (largely unsuccessful) quests to locate.

To learn more about campsite availability and fees, lake access points, and trail maps, contact the Angelina National Forest park office (111 Walnut Ridge Rd. in Zavalla, 936/897-1068, www.fs.fed.us/r8/texas, Mon.–Fri. 8 A.M.–4:30 P.M.).

Davy Crockett National Forest

Like to hike? Then the Davy Crockett National Forest's wild frontier is right up your trail. With

Davy Crockett National Forest in East Texas

© TEXAS HISTORICAL COMMISSION

more than 160,000 acres of scenic woodlands just west of Lufkin, the Davy Crockett forest has some of the region's best opportunities for hiking and horseback riding.

Most popular among bipeds is the Four C National Recreation Trail, named after the Central Coal and Coke Company that logged the forest's stately trees from 1902 to 1920. The 20-mile trail traverses moderate terrain amid lofty pines, swampy bogs, and hardwood forests. Horses and hikers share the woodsy, mossy, and boggy 50-mile Piney Creek Horse Trail.

Visitors are also drawn to the Ratcliff Lake Recreation Area, built in 1936 by the Civilian Conservation Corps around a 45-acre lake that was once a log pond and source of water for the Central Coal and Coke Company Sawmill. The area offers camping, a swimming beach and bathhouse, interpretive trail, showers, boating, and fishing.

Camping is also available along the Four C trail at the Walnut Creek campsite (five tent pads, a shelter, and pit toilet) and at another small campsite, farther north on the trail, with two tent pads. Campers comfortable with primitive sites should head to the nearby Neches Bluff Overlook at the north end of the trail, where they can enjoy a panoramic view of pine-hardwood forests in the Neches River bottomlands.

While hiking, be on the lookout for the forest's abundant wildlife, including deer, turkey, dove, quail, and various waterfowl. The endangered red-cockaded woodpecker also lives in a managed habitat within the forest.

To obtain a map or to learn more about camping and boat accessibility, contact the Davy Crockett National Forest headquarters near Kennard at Route 1, Box 55 FS (936/655-2299). To find out more about the forest and its seasonal activities, visit www.fs.fed.us/r8/texas. The ranger district office is located near Ratcliff on Highway 7, approximately 0.25 mile west of FM 227.

Sabine National Forest

The 160,656-acre Sabine National Forest is the easternmost of Texas's four national forests and is dominated by the massive Toledo Bend Reservoir along the Louisiana border.

Considered the second-largest lake in Texas and the fifth-largest man-made reservoir in the United States, Toledo Bend offers extensive recreational opportunities, from boating and fishing to swimming and lakeshore camping. For a comprehensive list of lake services—fishing guides to private resorts to boat launch sites—visit www.toledo-bend.com.

Outdoor recreation opportunities in the Sabine National Forest include fishing, hunting, camping, hiking, horseback riding, and mountain biking. One of the most popular destinations in the forest is the 12,369-acre Indian Mounds Wilderness Area, designated by the U.S. Congress as a site "to allow the Earth's natural processes to shape and influence the area." Unfortunately, it was misnamed since the mounds are actually just normal hills; fortunately, these natural formations shelter beautiful flora, including American beech, southern magnolia, yellow lady's slipper orchids, and broad beech ferns.

Less primitive is the Ragtown Recreation Area, offering opportunities for hiking, fishing, and bird-watching atop a bluff that facing the lake. Camping with electrical hookups is available only at Red Hills Lake and Boles Field.

Hikers should hoof it to the 28-mile Trail Between the Lakes, extending from the Toledo Bend Reservoir's Lakeview Recreation Area to Highway 96 near Sam Rayburn Reservoir. Contact park headquarters for a map showing the many miles of roads throughout the forest that are open to mountain bikers and horseback riders.

Anglers have many opportunities for fishing, and although the massive reservoir seems to be the best spot to catch large volumes of big fish (a striped bass fishery on Toledo Bend spawns fish reaching upward of 30 pounds), it's the forest's rivers and creeks that draw many recreational anglers. Crappie, bass, and bluegill are prevalent in the upper Sabine River, and the approximately 18 miles of perennial

Sabine National Forest

streams in the forest support populations of warm-water fish.

Birding is also popular with forest visitors, who flock to the area during the spring and fall to catch a glimpse of migratory waterfowl and other species of neotropical migratory birds such as songbirds, hawks, and shorebirds. Like the other East Texas forests, the red-cockaded woodpecker, an endangered species, receives special habitat management.

To learn more about campsite availability and fees, lake access points, and trail maps, contact the Sabine National Forest headquarters at 201 South Palm in Hemphill (409/787-3870). To learn more about the park's recreational opportunities and seasonal news, visit www. fs.fed.us/r8/texas.

Sam Houston National Forest

Located approximately 40 miles north of Texas's largest city, Sam Houston National Forest contains 162,984 acres of short- and long-leafed pine, hardwood forests, and abundant recreational opportunities appealing to visitors, big-city dwellers, and small-town folk. Camping is the main draw here, complemented by daytime activities on Double Lake and Lake Conroe and the 140-mile-long Lone Star Hiking Trail.

Sam Houston National Forest contains three developed campgrounds (Cagle, Double Lake, and Stubblefield Recreation Areas). Cagle Recreation Area is a campground with 48 camping units offering electric, water, and sewer connections; hot showers; lakeshore hiking, biking, and equestrian trails; fishing; and swimming. Double Lake Recreation Area, constructed in 1937 by the Civilian Conservation Corps, surrounds a 24-acre lake and includes family camping units (a tent pad, parking area, picnic table; some with water, sewer, and electrical hookups), swimming area and beach, and a concession stand with bathhouse. Stubblefield Recreation Area has 28 camping units, hot showers, and access to fishing and hiking. Double Lake facilities are available by reservations, while Cagle and Stubblefield are available on a first-come, first-served basis only.

For reservation information, call 877/444-6777 or go to www.recreation.gov.

The Lone Star Hiking Trail contains approximately 140 miles of walkways open to foot travel only. The trail traverses the entire Sam Houston National Forest through woodlands, swamps, and meadows via five loops to accommodate various starting points and parking for day hikers or overnight backpackers. Trail maps and brochures are available at the park headquarters in New Waverly (contact information follows).

Cyclists will enjoy the eight-mile trail on the east side of the forest custom built by mountain bikers. Though most of the East Texas forests are devoid of significant slopes, this hilly trek offers terrain-filled passages winding through the pine forests.

The 22,000-acre Lake Conroe is one of the biggest draws to Sam Houston forest, particularly for its swimming, boating, fishing, and sailing. The lake is stocked with bass and bluegill, and boats are available for rent at various marinas along the lakeshore.

For more information about recreational opportunities at the forest, including all-important maps, contact the headquarters, located two miles west of I-45 and New Waverly at 394 FM 1375 (936/344-6205 or 888/361-6908, www.fs.fed.us/r8/texas, Mon.–Fri. 8 A.M.–4:30 P.M.).

ALABAMA-COUSHATTA INDIAN RESERVATION

One of only three Indian reservations in Texas, the Alabama-Coushatta reservation represents the distinctive heritage of this small yet proud group. At one time the tribe offered tours, a museum, and cultural events for tourists; unfortunately, they are no longer operating. Regardless, visitors are encouraged to spend time at the reservation's campground or fishing on Lake Tombigbee (information follows).

Located on 4,600 acres of dense woodland close to the center of the Big Thicket National Preserve, the Alabama-Coushatta reservation was established in 1854 by Sam Houston as a reward to the tribes for their courage in remaining

neutral during the Texas War for Independence from Mexico. Both groups had been living in the Big Thicket area since circa 1800, when they migrated westward to hunt and build homes out of the abundant East Texas timber.

White settlers displaced countless tribe members, prompting many Coushattas to relocate near Kinder, Louisiana, where a majority still resides today. Malnutrition and disease took their toll on the Alabama-Coushatta, resulting in a disturbingly low population of 200 members in the late 1800s.

By the 1920s, the state and federal government recognized their poor living conditions and appropriated funds to purchase additional land, construct frame houses to replace meager log cabins, dig wells to help eliminate long water treks to natural springs, and provide medical and educational resources.

Despite the closing of the tribe's cultural facilities, the reservation still operates the popular Lake Tombigbee Campground, offering primitive sites, full-capacity RV stations, restrooms with bathhouses, swimming areas, and hiking and nature trails.

Call 936/563-1221 or 800/926-9038 for camping information and to obtain a map of the facilities. For additional information about the tribe, call 936/563-1100 or visit their well-organized and regularly updated website: www.alabama-coushatta.com.

LUFKIN

Lufkin (population 33,863) is worth visiting for its unique role as a major logging town in Texas's history. Founded in 1882 as a stop on the Houston, East and West Texas Railway, the town was named for Abraham P. Lufkin, a Galveston cotton merchant and close friend of the railroad company president.

The construction of railroad lines in the early 1880s allowed access to the forests' interiors, and the lumber industry and regional economy began to flourish. In fact, between 1890 and 1900, the forest industry contributed more to Texas's economy than any other industry, including the traditional stronghold markets of cattle and cotton.

As a result, lumber "company towns" flourished in the Lufkin area. The corporations provided jobs for men and prioritized family life by building and advocating schools, churches, and medical facilities. Often, the workers were paid in coupons and credits redeemable for merchandise and services in the company town facilities. Although some sawmill workers were later drawn to the oil fields for higher wages, many men chose to stay with their families in the lumber company towns since they were good places to raise a family in a community environment.

The lumber industry continues to play a significant role in Lufkin's economy. Each year, the region produces more than a million board feet of saw timber as well as a significant manufacturing of pulpwood from the nearby pine and hardwood forests.

Visitors, especially antiques shoppers and history buffs, are drawn to downtown Lufkin's quaint mix of restaurants and retail shops. A walking tour showcases several remarkable historic buildings, including the 1925 Pines Theater and the location of the first Brookshire Brothers grocery store. Along the way, look for the five colorful murals by artist Lance Hunter depicting historic businesses and stories from the area.

Texas Forestry Museum

An essential stop in Lufkin is the incomparable Texas Forestry Museum (1905 Atkinson Dr., 936/632-9535, www.treetexas.com, Mon.–Sat. 10 A.M.–5 P.M., Sun. 1–5 P.M., free admission). The museum offers a look at historic and contemporary growth of the region's lumber industry in two main areas—the forest history wing and resource/management wing.

Highlights include a compelling exhibit about life in a lumber company town, complete with model buildings and a large collection of artifacts from early logging camps. Historic equipment, a fire lookout tower cab, paper mill room, and an educational exhibit detailing the natural succession of a forest are other noteworthy attractions at the Texas Forestry Museum. Visitors can learn more about the region's natural resources on the scenic Urban Wildscape Trail located behind the main building.

Museum of East Texas

Despite its all-encompassing name, the Museum of East Texas (503 N. 2nd St., 936/639-4434, Tues.–Fri. 9 A.M.–5 P.M., Sat. and Sun. 1–5 P.M., free admission) isn't as grand as it sounds. Built in 1976, the museum primarily features exhibits showcasing the talents of regional artists. Though there are occasional traveling shows and science or children's exhibits, the museum devotes much of its attention to the work of locals, which is certainly commendable yet somewhat limited in scope. The museum also hosts occasional lectures, performances, classes, kids' art camps, and publications dedicated to the character and heritage of East Texas.

The History Center

Located just 11 miles outside Lufkin in the small town of Diboll is a fascinating attraction known simply as The History Center (102 N. Temple St., 936/829-3543, www.thehistorycenteronline.com, Mon.–Fri. 8 A.M.–5 P.M., Sat. 9 A.M.–1 P.M., free admission). Appropriately situated in Diboll, the oldest continually operated forest company site in Texas, the 12,000-square-foot History Center is technically a public archives facility dedicated to East Texas history. But that makes it sound rather boring, which it's not.

The vaguely named History Center did not get a specified moniker because organizers did not want it to be classified as simply a museum or a library. Although it contains many reference materials, it's more than a research center. Likewise, it features artifacts, but it is not really a museum. It's best described as a public history and archive center that collects, preserves, and explores the heritage of East Texas.

Visitors are immediately drawn to the facility by its exquisite woodwork, consisting of cypress walls preserved from the 1950s along with floors of locally harvested yellow pine. Exhibit panels feature remarkable century-old photos showcasing Diboll's dynamic past as a lumber company town, an impressive collection of archives (including 70,000 photos, decades' worth of community newspapers, lumber company log books), and an authentic 1920 Baldwin 68-ton steam locomotive where kids and adults can climb aboard to experience the immense satisfaction of sounding the authentic steam whistle.

Accommodations

Lufkin's lodging options are somewhat limited, but there are several chains offering reliable accommodations and amenities. Those looking for an affordable rate in a commendable hotel should consider **La Quinta** (2119 S. 1st St., 936/634-3351, www.lq.com, $95 d). Features include an outdoor pool, free continental breakfast, and free Internet access. A step up on the price and quality ladder is **Best Western Crown Colony Inn & Suites** (3211 S. 1st St., 936/634-3481, www.bestwesterntexas.com, $109 d), offering spacious rooms with microwaves and refrigerators, free Internet access, a deluxe continental breakfast, outdoor pool, and fitness room. Similar in price and scope is **Hampton Inn & Suites** (4400 S. 1st St., 936/699-2500, www.hamptoninn.com, $139 d), featuring a free hot breakfast, to-go breakfast bags (on weekdays), and free Internet access.

A suggested alternative to the chain hotels is the welcoming **Wisteria Hideaway** (3458 Ted Trout Dr., 936/875-2914, www.wisteriahideaway.com, rooms start at $95). Located in a 1939 Colonial-style home, this B&B provides genuinely charming Southern hospitality without being too fancy. Or frilly. Rooms are tastefully decorated, and the breakfasts are outstanding, starting with the freshly made buttermilk biscuits and continuing with fluffy and flavorful egg casseroles and sausage or bacon. Enjoy the feast in the dining room or the privacy of your own quarters.

Food
AMERICAN

Like most small towns in Texas and across the United States, Lufkin has many generic chains and a few admirable local down-home eateries. One of the most popular is **Mom's Diner** (900 W. Frank Ave., 936/637-6410, $6–14). As its name implies, this semirustic spot specializes in comfort food, including one of the best chicken-fried steaks in the area, as well as juicy burgers, fried chicken, and outstanding peppered cream gravy. Take note: Mom doesn't accept credit cards, just cash.

For old-time greasy and tasty burgers, head to **Ray's Drive In Cafe** (420 N. Timberland Dr., 936/634-3262, $5–9). Locals love the classic '50s feel and fare of this original drive-in restaurant, including the mouthwatering bacon cheeseburger with onion rings, mushroom burger, chili dog, and chocolate milk shake. The surrounding sound of classic oldies music completes this nostalgic scene.

BARBECUE

To experience a classic East Texas barbecue joint, go directly to **Bryan's Smokehouse Bar-B-Q** (609 S. Timberland Dr., 936/632-2255, $8–17). This small, rustic smokehouse has everything a barbecue place should— smoke-stained photos of local and regional musicians, hearty portions of succulent meat, and a sticky, tangy sauce. Brisket and pork ribs are the favorites here, and you can't go wrong with the better-than-average sides, particularly the savory beans and sweet potato salad. For those feeling adventurous, give the fried cabbage a try. **Lufkin Bar B Q** (203 S. Chestnut St., 936/634-4744, $8–17) isn't quite as strong on character, but the food is nearly as good. Tasty brisket and spicy sausage are the way to go, or try a chipped beef sandwich if you're not in the mood for quantity. The sides here are rather average, but a cold Dr Pepper will always enhance your meal.

MEXICAN

Lufkin is known more for its barbecue than Mexican food, but there are several places in town that draw sizable lunch crowds. One worth visiting is the consistently reliable **Cafe Del Rio** (1901 S. 1st St., 936/639-4471, $7–15). From the crispy chips and spicy salsa to the loaded nachos and sizzling fajitas, Cafe Del Rio doesn't disappoint. Also recommended is **Casa Ole** (2109 S. 1st St., 936/632-2653, $6–14), offering tasty tacos and hearty enchiladas. Another local hot spot is **El Taurino Mexican Grill** (3774 Hwy. 69 N., 936/699-3344, www.eltaurinomexicanrestaurant.com, $5–14), featuring classic Mexican combo dishes with enchiladas, tacos, chiles rellenos, and burritos.

Information and Services

To get the scoop on additional lodging and dining options or to pick up a handy map or brochure, stop by the **Lufkin Convention & Visitors Bureau** (1615 S. Chestnut St., 936/633-0349 or 800/409-5659, www.visitlufkin.com, Mon.–Fri. 8:30 A.M.–5 P.M.).

NACOGDOCHES AND VICINITY

Nacogdoches (population 31,135) claims to be Texas's oldest town, and though some historians debate this, there's no denying the wealth and breadth of its East Texas heritage and culture.

Named for the Caddo tribe (the Nacogdoche) that lived in the area, Nacogdoches was an active Native American settlement until 1716 when Spain established a mission at the site. In 1779, Nacogdoches received official designation from Spain as a pueblo (village), prompting locals to deem it Texas's first official "town."

Soon after, Nacogdoches became a hotbed of trading activity, most of it illicit, primarily among the French and Americans, with much of the action centered around the Old Stone Fort. The frequent activity coupled with the town's prime location on several major trade routes made Nacogdoches prominent in early military and political arenas.

By the mid-1800s, Nacogdoches lost its distinction in these areas due to its lack of modern transportation facilities such as steamboats and railroads. Growth remained relatively stagnant until the 1920s, when Stephen F. Austin State Teachers College (now Stephen F. Austin State University) opened its doors, bringing fresh

faces, jobs, and cultural activities to town. With a current enrollment of nearly 12,000 students, the university remains the lifeblood of Nacogdoches.

Old Stone Fort Museum

The Old Stone Fort Museum (1936 North St., 936/468-2408, www.sfasu.edu/stonefort, Tues.–Sat. 9 A.M.–5 P.M., Sun. 1–5 P.M., free admission), located on the Stephen F. Austin State University campus, is a 1936 replica of the home of Don Antonio Gil Y'Barbo, considered the founder of present-day Nacogdoches. The original facility, dating to the 1700s, was considered the oldest standing stone structure in Texas before it was torn down amid much protest in 1902. Now officially historic itself, this replica remains an important Nacogdoches landmark, featuring a permanent exhibit on the fascinating history of the building that served as a trading post, church, jail, private home, and saloon but never an official fort. The Old Stone Fort Museum also contains artifacts related to the early history of East Texas, with a special focus on the Spanish and Mexican periods (1690–1836).

Sterne-Hoya House

One of the oldest homes in East Texas is the 1830 Sterne-Hoya House (211 S. Lanana St., 936/560-5426, Tues.–Sat. 10 A.M.–4 P.M., free admission and tours). Built by Adolphus Sterne, a prominent leader of the Texas Revolution, the modest yet stately home is still standing on its original site, a rare claim for many structures of this era, which were either moved or demolished. Prominent figures of the time, including Davy Crockett, Sam Houston, and Cherokee chief Bowles, visited the Sterne home in the mid-1800s. Tour guides explain the significance of the period antiques and the prominent families who occupied the home, which is now listed on the National Register of Historic Places.

Stephen F. Austin Experimental Forest

Looking for a quiet retreat to the surrounding

woodlands? Then hoof it to the Stephen F. Austin Experimental Forest (eight miles southwest of Nacogdoches at 6598 FM 2782, 936/564-8924, www.srs.fs.usda.gov). Not quite as compelling at its name implies, the forest is dubbed "experimental" for its crazy variety of tree species planted in the 1940s. A century ago, the area was logged and abandoned for use as cotton fields, but the U.S. government's purchase of more than 600,000 acres of East Texas property—eventually becoming the region's national forests—allowed for the reforestation of hardwoods and pines that would eventually populate the area. The Experimental Forest contains three miles of trails with interpretive signs. Visitors and locals regularly traverse the wooded trails to catch a glimpse of the more than 150 species of birds and 80 kinds of butterflies throughout this peaceful site.

◖ Texas State Railroad

The rich throaty sound of a steam train whistle beckons visitors to the Texas State Railroad

(Park Rd. 76 off Hwy. 84 W., 888/987-2461, www.texasstaterr.com). The nearest depot is located in Rusk, approximately 30 miles northwest of Nacogdoches, where passengers get all aboard on a historic journey through the East Texas Piney Woods. Trains have rolled on these 25 miles of rustic yet sturdy tracks between Rusk and Palestine since 1881, when the state prison system began constructing the railway to transport iron ore and timber.

The 90-minute trek between the two towns is a thoroughly enjoyable and relaxing journey into the past, with gently rolling train cars clickety-clacking over bridges and through the dense green forest. Sit back and let time slowly slip by while the steam locomotive's whistle bellows and the genial conductor checks your ticket. Before you know it, you'll be at the Victorian-style depot at the end of the line, where you'll find historical exhibits, gift shops, and food service.

Round-trip excursions depart each weekend year-round from both the Rusk and Palestine depots at 11 A.M. and return to their point of

the Texas State Railroad

origin by 3:30 P.M. Adult tickets run $36.50, and child (ages 3–11) fares are $19. A 90-minute layover is scheduled at the opposite train depot, where a variety of lunch options are available. Snacks, beverages, and restrooms are provided on the train.

Caddo Mounds State Historic Site

Just south of Rusk near the small town of Alto is the compelling Caddo Mounds State Historic Site (1649 State Hwy. 21 W., 936/858-3218, www.visitcaddomounds.com, Tues.–Sun. 8:30 A.M.–4:30 P.M., $4 adults, $3 students). Caddo-speaking farmers built these ceremonial burial mounds more than 1,200 years ago, and historians now realize they are the southwestern-most structures of the legendary Mound Builders of the eastern North American woodlands. Three of these earthen mounds, used for burials, temples, and religious ceremonies, still

rise from the East Texas forests. Visitors can walk among the gently sloping structures, explore the interpretive center's exhibits and displays, and view a reconstructed Caddo house built with Stone Age tools.

Accommodations

Like Lufkin, Nacogdoches's lodging options are primarily chains, with most located near the Stephen F. Austin campus. The best budget choice is **Best Western Inn of Nacogdoches** (3428 South St., 936/560-4900, www.bestwestern.com, $85 d), offering rooms with free Internet access along with microwaves and refrigerators, a free continental breakfast, and an outdoor pool. One of Nacogdoches's few locally run establishments is the pleasant downtown six-story **Fredonia** (200 N. Fredonia St., 936/564-1234, www.fredoniahotel.com, $89 d). In operation since 1955, the Fredonia features Wi-Fi access, a large outdoor pool, and a fitness center.

CADDO COMMUNITIES

Most of East Texas was originally occupied by the remarkable Caddo Indians, a large tribe consisting of dozens of distinct groups or "families" occupying an enormous area covering portions of modern-day Texas, Oklahoma, Arkansas, and Louisiana.

When Europeans first arrived in the 1500s and 1600s, they encountered many Caddo communities along streams and rivers. The tribe members were farmers who grew corn, beans, squash, sunflowers, and other crops that flourished in the humid and semirainy East Texas environment.

Although the Caddo people were in remote river and stream valleys, their tribal leaders usually lived in larger villages, where tall temples built of poles and thatched grass often stood atop earthen mounds. These were ritualistic centers where tribe members gathered for festive activities or during times of crisis.

The vast territory occupied by the Caddo provided them much protection, but they also had a reputation as fierce and skillful warriors.

When threatened, the groups would band together and form a formidable force.

The Caddo were also known for their pottery skills. Caddo women made everything from three-foot-tall storage jars to tiny bowls as well as smoking pipes and earspools. In addition to pottery and wooden bowls, the Caddo traded buffalo hides and horses for French guns and merchandise.

Today, descendants of this great group make up the Caddo Nation of Oklahoma, with nearly 4,000 members on its official tribal roll. The tribe's headquarters is approximately 45 miles west of Oklahoma City in the town of Binger.

In Texas, a 1,200-year-old village and ceremonial site now known as Caddo Mounds State Historic Site was once the southwestern-most ceremonial center for the tribe. Three earthen mounds still rise from the East Texas landscape near the small town of Alto, where visitors can learn about the everyday lives and heritage of this ancient civilization. For more information, call 936-858-3218 or visit www.visitcaddomounds.com.

Moving into the triple-digit range is the clean and comfortable **Holiday Inn Express Hotel & Suites** (3807 South St., 936/564-0100, www.hiexpress.com, $109 d), with amenities such as free wireless Internet service, a fancy fitness center, and an outdoor pool. A popular option with business travelers is the nearby **Hampton Inn & Suites** (3625 South St., 936/560-9901, www.hamptoninn.com, $119 d), offering free Internet access, a complimentary hot breakfast buffet, an outdoor pool, and a fitness center.

Food
AMERICAN
If you're in the downtown area at lunch, drop by the wonderful **Shelly's Bakery Cafe** (112 N. Church St., 936/564-4100, www.shellys-bakerycafe.com, closed Sun. and Mon., $5–14). The salads are a big draw here, as are the hearty sandwiches. Billing itself as a European-style Bistro, Shelley's is one of those tucked-away little places that's ideal for grabbing a midmorning coffee and pastry while perusing the local paper. Another popular lunch spot is the campus-area **Stacy's Deli** (3205 N. University Dr., 936/564-3588, closed Sun., $4–8). Students and professors line up at this shopping-center deli for tasty BLTs, Reubens, and meatball subs accompanied by salty chips and a large iced tea. Stacy's spicy pickles are legendary among SFASU students. Locals also love the regional chain **Clear Springs Cafe** (211 Old Tyler Rd., 936/569-0489, www.clear-springsrestaurant.com, $6–19). Seafood is the main draw here, including popular dishes such as the pan-seared tilapia, salmon or crawfish salad, and catfish étouffée.

BARBECUE
Don't let the shiny new decor fool you at the **Barbecue House** (704 N. Stallings Dr., 936/569-9004, cash only, $8–16). Just because the building is new, it doesn't mean the food is fancy. This is classic East Texas–style barbecue done right: sweet tomato-based sauce smothering delicious brisket, savory sausage, and meaty pork ribs. Instead of pinto beans and coleslaw,

opt for the red beans and rice. Houston-based **Harlon's Bar B Que** (603 Old Tyler Rd., 936/564-4850, $7–14) isn't quite as tantalizing, but it'll satisfy your craving. The brisket and chicken are popular here, as are the weekend late-night gatherings, where blues music, karaoke, and dancing are often on the menu.

MEXICAN
Nacogdoches isn't really known for its quality Mexican restaurants, but there are a couple options in town if you need a fajita fix. **San Miguel Mexican Restaurant** (2524 South St., 936/569-2082, $6–15) offers all the classics: chicken enchiladas with green sauce, tacos, burritos, and even fried ice cream. Another option is **Restaurant El Ranchero** (123 King St., 936/569-2256, $7–14), featuring some of the hottest and heartiest salsa in town, along with traditional favorites such as quesadillas, fajitas, and flautas. Call in advance to see if they're offering their semiregular "two free margaritas" special.

Information and Services
While strolling historic downtown Nacogdoches, drop by the town's two main tourism offices. The **Nacogdoches Convention & Visitors Bureau** (200 E. Main St., 888/653-3788, www.visitnacogdoches.org, Mon.–Fri. 9 A.M.–5 P.M., Sat. 10 A.M.–4 P.M., Sun. 1–4 P.M.) to learn about the city's history and to pick up information on local sites of interest. Just around the corner is the office headquarters of the **Texas Forest Trail Region** (202 E. Pilar St., 936/560-3699, www.texas-foresttrail.com, Mon.–Fri. 8:30 A.M.–5 P.M.). Operated by the Texas Historical Commission, the Forest Trail Region oversees heritage travel destinations and cultural activities in Nacogdoches and the entire East Texas Piney Woods region. Drop by to pick up brochures, maps, and to talk to the friendly and knowledgeable staff.

TYLER
Slow-moving Tyler will never be confused with fast-paced Austin, but this large town/

HOUSTON AND EAST TEXAS

TYLER

downtown Tyler

© TEXAS HISTORICAL COMMISSION

small city (population 94,146) certainly has a distinctive feel: Southern. From stately plantations to hospitable residents to deep-fried cooking, Tyler has a strong cultural connection to the Deep South.

The city's biggest draw is its roses. Once responsible for more than half of the country's rose bush supply, Tyler now provides 20 percent of the roses in the United States. The Tyler Municipal Rose Garden contains more than 35,000 rosebushes representing nearly 500 varieties. The gardens attract bees, butterflies, and more than 100,000 people annually from across the world. Many visitors come especially for the Texas Rose Festival, a tradition held each October since 1933, featuring events such as the queen's coronation, the rose parade, the queen's tea, and the rose show.

Tyler changed dramatically in 1930, when the discovery of the nearby East Texas oil field turned this small agricultural and railroad city into a major destination for workers and corporations. The town received an added boost in the 1940s when Camp Fannin was established

nearby, including a troop capacity of 19,000 at the height of World War II.

In the following decades, Tyler's economic base shifted from agriculture to industry. Most were petroleum related, but other manufacturing plants soon followed, including metal and fabricating companies, railroad and machine shops, furniture and woodwork manufacturers, aluminum foundries, and air-conditioning and refrigeration plants.

In the 1970s and '80s, Tyler was best known as the hometown of football legend Earl Campbell, who earned the Heisman Trophy at the University of Texas and went on to become a Hall of Fame running back in the National Football League. Campbell's nickname, "The Tyler Rose," forever linked him with his hometown.

Tyler Municipal Rose Garden and Museum

The region's most popular tourist attraction is the Tyler Municipal Rose Garden and Museum (420 Rose Park Dr., 903/597-3130,

BOOM! GOES THE TOWN

In the early 1900s, East Texas was a land of opportunity, with prospectors speculating about the location of the next big oil field. More often than not, their efforts were unsuccessful. But when they guessed correctly and tapped into a fertile patch of petroleum, the fortunes of everyone associated with the discovery exploded like the gusher of oil that burst into the East Texas sky.

The wildcatters working at the base of Beaumont's Lucas gusher certainly couldn't have predicted the global impact they'd helped create on January 10, 1901. Once word spread about the gusher's subterranean Spindletop oil field, tens of thousands of people flocked to Beaumont to make their fortunes.

Everyone wanted a piece of the action, from engineers and riggers to real estate companies and saloon owners. Virtually overnight, the oil discovery transformed Beaumont from a small village of several hundred rice farmers and cattle raisers to a big ol' boomtown of petroleum barons, field workers, and the people who provided services to them.

A lesser-known East Texas boomtown was Kilgore, about 30 miles east of Tyler. Kilgore's glory years began in 1930, when the first oil gusher arrived; within weeks, the town's population surged from 500 people to more than 10,000. Before well-spacing regulations were adopted, Kilgore boasted a small section of downtown that became known as the "World's Richest Acre," where 24 oil wells once stood.

At the height of Kilgore's boom, residents woke up to find their yards filled with strangers covered with boxes, sacks, and newspapers. People installed iron doors on their homes for protection from the influx of newcomers, and they stopped hanging their clothes out to dry since they'd be stolen right off the line.

Not surprisingly, the oil boom also brought professional undesirables such as con men, criminals, and prostitutes to these small East Texas towns. The Texas Rangers were assigned to clean up the area, and they often had to resort to unorthodox means – like the time they "remodeled" an old church into a makeshift prison with padlocked prisoners lining the interior walls – to address the newfound population of ne'er-do-wells.

These stories, along with photos and artifacts, are often on display at local history museums in East Texas. For a full-fledged step back in time to the region's oil boomtown glory years, visit Kilgore's comprehensive and compelling **East Texas Oil Museum** (at the intersection of Hwy. 259 and Ross St., 903/983-8295, www.easttexasoilmuseum.com, Tues.-Sat. 9 A.M.-4 P.M., Sun. 2 P.M.-5 P.M., free admission).

---

www.texasrosefestival.com, Mon.–Fri. 9 A.M.–4:30 P.M., Sat. 10 A.M.–4:30 P.M., Sun. 1:30–4:30 P.M., $3.50 adults, $2 children ages 3–11). The museum is well worth visiting, with numerous displays showcasing the elaborately jeweled, hand-sewn gowns worn by rose queens dating back to 1935. Be sure to check out the scrapbook pages from each rose queen, including memorabilia, personal recollections, and photos (including one with a queen and her freshly killed deer). Visitors can also view videos about the history of Tyler's rose industry and rose festival, and experience an interactive "attic" exhibit with a bizarre collection of antiques and collectibles from Tyler's past.

The municipal garden is the primary draw, however, with its sea of colorful roses—more than 35,000 bushes representing the nearly 500 distinct varieties. Though the blooming period is from May through November, early May is the peak of the flowers' natural growing cycle. This is when the garden's 14 acres burst with the bright sight and sweet scent of fresh roses.

Plantation Museums

Tyler's heritage is on full display at Tyler's three plantation museums, where the Old South comes to life through historic furniture, artifacts, and photos. This lifestyle, typically associated with the Deep South, wasn't prevalent in most of Texas, so it's worth dropping by one of these sites just to get a feel for the ornate homes and luxurious grounds. If you're lucky, the docents and tour guides may even be dressed in period costume.

The Goodman Museum (624 N. Broadway Ave., 903/531-1286, www.cityoftyler.org, Tues.–Sat. 10 A.M.–4 P.M., free admission) was the home of Dr. W. J. Goodman, a local doctor and Civil War surgeon for 72 years (1866–1938). Originally built in 1859, the house is Tyler's first property to be listed on the National Register of Historic Places. The museum features original furnishings, including hand-carved tables and chairs, a grandfather clock from the colonial era, surgical tools and medical cases, and fine silver and china. It's open for walk-in tours.

Just as impressive is the 1854 **Dewberry Plantation** (14007 FM 346 W., 903/825-9000, www.dewberryplantation.com, open daily, tours are $8 adults, $7 seniors, $5 children ages 6–18). The plantation site served as a campground for the officers of the Army of Republic of Texas prior to their final battle with the Cherokee Indians. The home, billed as the only original two-story, pre–Civil War house still standing in Smith County, was built for War of 1812 hero Col. John Dewberry, who moved to the Tyler area in 1835.

Also noteworthy is the grand 1878 **McClendon House** (806 W. Houston St., 903/592-3533, www.mcclendonhouse.net, Tues.–Sat. 10 A.M.–5 P.M., tours $5). Once a hub for Tyler's eloquent Victorian society, the home was eventually purchased by the McClendon family, whose youngest daughter, Sarah, became a noted Washington, D.C., journalist with a presidential-coverage career spanning from Franklin Roosevelt to George W. Bush. The home is now primarily used as a wedding and events site, but is open to the public for tours. Drop-in tours should check in first at the adjacent Gipson Girl (625 Vine Street).

Caldwell Zoo

Big cities don't necessarily have the best zoos.

One of the best-run and highly acclaimed zoos in the state is Tyler's Caldwell Zoo (2203 W. Martin Luther King Jr. Blvd., 903/593-0121, www.caldwellzoo.org, 9 A.M.–5 P.M. daily Mar. 1–Labor Day, 9 A.M.–4 P.M. daily in the off-season, $8.50 adults ages 13–54, $7.25 seniors, $5 children ages 3–12). What started in 1938 as a backyard menagerie of squirrels and parrots for schoolchildren has evolved into an 85-acre zoo containing more than 2,000 animals representing species from East Africa, North America, and South America. Animals on display in naturalistic habitats include monkeys, rhinos, elephants, giraffes, cheetahs, and mountain lions.

Tyler Museum of Art

For a dose of traditional culture, visit the respectable Tyler Museum of Art (located on the east side of the Tyler Junior College campus at 1300 South Mahon Ave., 903/595-1001, www.tylermuseum.org, Tues.–Sat. 10 A.M.–5 P.M., Sun. 1–5 P.M., $7 adults, $5 seniors and students). The museum primarily showcases local and regional artists with an emphasis on contemporary works; however, occasional traveling exhibits feature centuries-old European paintings, Japanese artwork, and Native American pottery and ceramics. It contains three galleries on the main level, a smaller gallery for special exhibits upstairs, and a children's gallery.

Accommodations

Chain hotels are pretty much the only choice in Tyler; fortunately, the available options are safe, reliable, and relatively affordable. On the lower end of the price spectrum is **Days Inn & Suites** (2739 W. Northwest Loop 323, 903/531-9513, www.daysinn.com, $65 d), offering some decent amenities, including a free breakfast, free Internet access, and a fitness center. **La Quinta** (1601 W. Southwest Loop 323, 903/561-2223, www.lq.com, $75 d) features free Internet access, a free continental breakfast, and an outdoor pool.

Perhaps the best deal in town is the **Comfort Suites at South Broadway Mall** (303 E. Rieck Rd., 903/534-0999, www.choicehotels.

com, $99 d), offering rooms with free Internet access, microwaves, and refrigerators, and hotel amenities such as an exercise room, free continental breakfast, manager's reception (free happy hour drinks), and an indoor heated pool and whirlpool. The only drawback is its location: too far south of the downtown activity.

A bit farther north, on Broadway and about 10 minutes from downtown, is the city's largest hotel—the comfortable **Holiday Inn Select** (5701 S. Broadway Ave., 903/561-5800 or 800/465-4329, www.holidayinn.com, $99 d). The Holiday Inn features free Wi-Fi service, an outdoor pool, a full-feature fitness center, and free meals for kids 12 and under.

Food

Tyler's quality restaurant options are better than you'd expect, particularly for a smallish city in a largely rural area of the state. Perhaps it's the steady arrival of Dallas retirees demanding fine-dining establishments, but the end result is good news for everyone, from travelers to locals to newcomers.

AMERICAN

A stalwart on the scene is ◖ **Rick's on the Square** (104 W. Erwin St., 903/531-2415, www.rix.com, $9–31), a swanky lunch and dinner joint and rowdy blues bar by night. Located in the heart of downtown in an old saloon and theater, Rick's is the kind of place that gets everything right—tempting appetizers (shrimp and oysters), gigantic juicy burgers with chunks of fried potatoes on the side, and exquisite entrées ranging from chicken dumplings to tortilla-crusted mahimahi to the indulgent yet highly recommended crawfish-stuffed filet mignon. Similar in approach menu-wise is the popular **Potpourri House** (3200 Troup Hwy., 903/592-4171, www.potpourrihouse. com, $8–27). This welcoming spot is combined with a retail establishment offering candles, antiques, jewelry, more candles, and probably even some potpourri. The restaurant's offerings range from club sandwiches to baked fish and chicken to prime rib.

A local legend and a must-experience for barbecue fans is **Stanley's Famous Pit Bar-B-Q** (525 S. Beckham Ave., 903/593-0311, www.stanleysfamous.com, $7–19). The smoked ribs here have been placed atop "best of" barbecue lists all across Texas, and for good reason—their tender, succulent taste will have you thinking about them for days. Try the smoked turkey and sausage, or sample a sliced brisket sandwich. Better yet, tackle the Brother-in-Law sandwich, teeming with sausage, chopped beef, and cheese.

MEXICAN

Tyler is pretty far away from the border, but that doesn't prevent it from having a few worthy Mexican restaurants. Among the most popular are the homegrown regional chains of Mercado's and Posado's.

If you're downtown, drop by **Posado's** (2500 E. 5th St., 903/597-2573, $6–14). The mission-style decor adds to the authentic Mexican taste, including interior-style dishes such as marinated quail fajitas and shrimp or fish platters. You can't go wrong with the classics here either, including chicken enchiladas and spicy beef tacos.

Locals also love **Taqueria El Lugar** (1920 1726 E. Gentry Pkwy., 903/597-4717, $6–15). As the name implies, tacos are the specialty here, and they're listed on the menu by number (up to 16). Order anything with the amazing guacamole and tasty beef (the cabbage isn't quite as recommendable), and be sure to ask for it on a corn tortilla.

Information and Services

The **Tyler Convention & Visitors Bureau** (315 N. Broadway Ave., 903/592-1661 or 800/235-5712, www.visittyler.com) is located just a few blocks north of the downtown square on the first floor of the historic Blackstone building. The friendly staffers will provide brochures, maps, and general information to help you get around the Rose Capital.

JEFFERSON

Jefferson (population 1,869) is nestled among the forests of far northeast Texas and certainly

ROSENWALD SCHOOLS

Rosenwald schools represent a brief yet far-reaching cultural phenomena that impacted the lives of thousands of underserved East Texans. These rural facilities were built throughout East Texas and the entire South in the early 1900s to benefit the African-American population thanks to Julius Rosenwald, a Chicago philanthropist and former president of Sears, Roebuck and Co.

Rosenwald felt compelled to address the educational needs of African-Americans in the rural South, who had previously attended makeshift schools in churches, shacks, and cabins. Rosenwald intended his facilities to serve as models of modern schoolhouse construction.

The Rosenwald program provided standardized-plan facilities that attracted qualified teachers and became community educational centers. These schools served as models for rural African-Americans to develop quality facilities and a better-educated population. To be comparable with the education in Anglo communities, Rosenwald required his schools to have certified college-educated teachers and a calendar year of at least five months. State and national funding paid for educational supplies, lesson plans, and, more importantly, additional high school levels. With the establishment of African-American colleges throughout the state, black students were able to complete 12 years of public school and go on to receive a college education, ultimately allowing them the freedom of working for themselves.

The last Texas Rosenwald building was constructed in 1931. School district consolidation and desegregation rendered most of the facilities obsolete by the late 1950s, but by that time, 527 Rosenwald schools had been built in Texas. Due to abandonment and neglect of these largely rural buildings, only 30 of them remain standing.

---

worth visiting for a pleasant escape to the Piney Woods' past. In its glory days of the mid-19th century, Jefferson was a burgeoning boomtown containing a kaleidoscope of cultures, from entrepreneurial East Coast shop merchants to newly freed slaves to Westward-moving pioneers. For more than a decade, Jefferson welcomed a steady flow of steamboats bringing worldly influences and people.

In 1870, Jefferson had a population of 4,180 and was the sixth-largest city in Texas. Between 1867 and 1870, steamboats became a tremendous factor in the town's commercial trade, which grew from $3 million to $8 million. By 1870, only the port of Galveston exceeded Jefferson in volume.

In 1873 things changed dramatically for Jefferson. The destruction of the Red River raft, a natural dam on the river, lowered the water level of the surrounding lakes and streams, making navigation to Jefferson via steamboat nearly impossible. Also that year, the Texas and Pacific Railway, which bypassed Jefferson, was completed. Without steamboat or railroad access, people started leaving Jefferson in droves.

In the mid-1900s, locals began looking at Jefferson's distinctive past as a way to preserve and promote the town's heritage, particularly its remarkable 100-plus state and nationally recognized historic structures. Known as the Bed and Breakfast Capital of Texas, tourism is now Jefferson's most important economic base.

Historic Buildings

With so much Southern heritage in such a small town, it's necessary to visit some of the sites that make Jefferson so historically significant. One of its crown jewels is the amazing **House of the Seasons** (409 S. Alley St., 903/665-8000, www.houseoftheseasons.com, tours available at 11 A.M. Mon.–Sat., $7.50 per person). Built in 1872 by Col. Benjamin Epperson, a prominent businessman and friend of Sam Houston, this magnificent home contains architectural elements representing styles ranging from Greek Revival to Italianate to Victorian. The house gets its name from the glass encasement on top of the house, featuring colored glass representing each season of the year.

A visit to Jefferson is incomplete without a stop at the fascinating **Jefferson General Store** (113 E. Austin St., 903/665 8481, www.jeffersongeneralstore.com, Sun.–Thurs. 9 A.M.–6 P.M., Fri.–Sat. 9 A.M.–10 P.M.). Walking through the creaky front screen doors offers a true step back in time, with vintage trinkets and current-day souvenirs mingling in a historic 1870s mercantile setting. Touches of bygone days are everywhere, from the signature five-cent cup of coffee to the homemade pecan pralines to the soda fountain. Jams, salsas, T-shirts, and candy round out this unique experience.

Also well worth a visit is **The Grove** (405 Moseley St., 903/665-8018, www.thegrove-jefferson.com, call for tour information, $6 admission). Referred to as "the most haunted house in Jefferson," The Grove is a private residence built in 1861 that was listed on the National Register of Historic Places. An hour-long tour offers a fascinating glimpse into the home, along with stories about the supernatural experiences of the owners, including a lady in a white dress who always takes the same path through the house when she appears. Its paranormal activity is so legendary, *This Old House* placed it on its list of Top 12 Haunted Homes, and it graces the cover of *A Texas Guide To Haunted Restaurants, Taverns, and Inns.*

Just outside of town is the stately **Freeman Plantation** (Hwy. 49 W., 903/665-2320), built on nearly 1,000 acres in 1850 by Williamson M. Freeman. Guided tours educate visitors about the Victorian antiques and the family who occupied the home during the antebellum period.

The Atalanta Railroad Car

The Atalanta (210 W. Austin St., 903/665-2513) was a private rail car used by railroad tycoon Jay Gould. It's rather odd that this elaborately designed and elegantly furnished car

ended up in Jefferson since the city rejected Gould's plans to bring a railroad through the town. Upon being spurned, he hightailed it out of there, predicting Jefferson's demise (he was partly right, since the town never regained its steamboat-era splendor of the 1860s). The Atalanta features nearly a dozen rooms containing opulent interior materials such as mahogany, crystal light fixtures, and silver bathroom accessories. Located downtown across from the Excelsior Hotel, it remains a major attraction in Jefferson's heritage tourism industry.

Scarlett O'Hardy's Gone With the Wind Museum

If you're still pining for historic ties to the Old South, drop by the campy and somewhat strange Scarlett O'Hardy's Gone With the Wind Museum (408 Taylor St., 903/665-1939, www.scarlettohardy.com, Thurs.–Sat. 10 A.M.–5 P.M., $3 adults, $1 children 12 and under). The jam-packed museum contains everything imaginable related to the classic film, including posters, photos, costume reproductions, dolls, and seats from the Atlanta theater where the movie premiered in 1939. Perhaps most interesting is the collection of autographs from the movie's stars, most notably Clark Gable and Vivien Leigh, Leslie Howard, Hattie McDaniel, and Butterfly McQueen.

Lake o' the Pines

The nearby Lake o' the Pines is just as charming as its name implies. This popular destination is particularly known for its fishing, with bass, catfish, and crappie the main biters. Recreational boating is another common activity, especially waterskiing, sailing, or relaxing on pontoon boats, party boats, and "floating cabins," all available at several lakeside marinas. Campers also flock to Lake o' the Pines, pitching tents and parking RVs at one of the four U.S. Army Corps of Engineer parks or privately owned campgrounds. Other options include guesthouses, cabins, or motels. For more information about lake services, contact the local chamber of commerce at www.lakeothepines.com or 903/755-2597.

◀ Caddo Lake

Just downriver from Jefferson is Caddo Lake, the only natural lake in Texas (all the others were created by dams). Stringy Spanish moss and outstretched cypress trees surround this mysteriously beautiful and sometimes-marshy lake. Caddo Indians claimed a giant flood formed the lake, but scientists believe massive logjams blocked the Red River, causing it to back up into the Cypress Bayou watershed, which formed the lake. Popular lake activities include camping, hiking, swimming, fishing, and boating. Among the many attractions at Caddo Lake is the Texas Parks and Wildlife–operated Caddo Lake State Park (take State Hwy. 43 to FM 2198, 903/679-3351, www. tpwd.state.tx.us). The park offers access to diverse fishing, canoe rentals, and quaint cabins, built by the Civilian Conservation Corps in the 1930s.

Accommodations

BED-AND-BREAKFASTS

Jefferson is the Bed and Breakfast Capital of Texas, so if you were ever going to stay in a B&B, this is the place to do it. It's practically required. The nearly 40 B&Bs far outnumber the measly hotel options, and the town is a Victorian-era playground, so you may as well go all the way.

Among the popular choices is the **Claiborne House Bed & Breakfast** (312 S. Alley, 903/665-8800, www.clairbornehousebnb. com, $119–179), a stately Greek Revival home built in 1872. The Claiborne House offers six rooms—four in the main house and two in the carriage house, each named after romantic poets (Yeats, Wilde, Dickinson, etc.). All rooms have a framed poem, book of the poet's work, wireless Internet access, private baths, and color TVs. A full Southern gourmet breakfast is served at 9 A.M., and a day spa is available featuring massages, body wraps, hot rock treatments, and salt scrubs.

Guests make regular returns to the remarkable **McKay House Bed & Breakfast Inn** (306 E. Delta St., 903/665-7322, www.mckayhouse.com, $139–149). The McKay house is famous for its attention to detail (Victorian nightgowns, sleep shirts, and period hats await on guests' beds) and its Gentleman's Breakfast (French toast, bacon, shirred eggs with ham, pineapple zucchini muffins, strawberry cheese blintzes). Seven rooms feature period furnishings, private baths, and Wi-Fi access, and the B&B provides lemonade, fireside coffee, a Packard pump organ, and a lush garden.

The **Old Mulberry Inn Bed & Breakfast** (209 Jefferson St., 903/665-1945, www.jeffersontexasinn.com, $89–169) is recommended by *Southern Living* magazine and even the *New York Times,* and for good reason. This antebellum home contains five guest rooms and two cottages with private baths featuring footed tubs, family heirlooms, cable TV, and free wireless Internet access. The three-course gourmet breakfasts include delectable items such as artichoke quiche, baked pears with cranberries, Rocky Mountain grits, and mulberry almond coffee cake.

HOTELS

For those who insist on staying in a normal plush-free hotel in the B&B Capital of Texas, there's really only one option in town: the independently owned **Inn of Jefferson** (400 S. Walcott St., 903/665-3983, www.hotel-jefferson.com, $89 d). There's nothing fancy about this place, but it's certainly pleasant, with a free full hot breakfast, an outdoor pool, and free 24-hour beverage service. A word of caution: The loud whistles from the trains across the highway can be quite distracting. Especially at 3 A.M.

The historic **Excelsior House** hotel (211 W. Austin St., 903/665-2513, www.theexcelsiorhouse.com, $119 d) is technically a hotel but feels like a B&B (not a surprise in this town). It's rich in history and ghosts, however, and has hosted guests since the 1850s. Fans of paranormal activity claim this is one of the most haunted locations in town. During Jefferson's prosperous days, famous people such as Ulysses S. Grant, Rutherford B, Hayes, and Oscar Wilde stayed here, and its 150-plus years of operation make it one of the oldest establishments of its kind still in business in Texas.

on about the coast, including
nd notices about current con-
s. The **Texas General Land**
each and Bay Access Guide
ironmental reports and down-
state.tx.us/coastal/access/), and
Coast Real Estate organization
a handy website with general
about coastal geology, beaches,
ap links (www.texasgulfcoaston-

G THERE
ROUND

elers arrive to the Gulf Coast by car
er locales within the state; however,
rvice is available via Corpus Christi
ional Airport and at Brownsville near
Padre.
e the majority of the coastline is unde-
d, there aren't any major freeways link-
ajor cities. State Highway 35 is the closest

option—a primarily rural road stretching between Houston and Corpus Christi passing
through dozens of small towns along the way.
The lengthy Padre Island National Seashore
is only accessible by a park road near Corpus
Christi; otherwise, the trek to South Padre
beaches is more than 20 miles offshore via U.S.
Highway 77 through Kingsville, Harlingen,
and Brownsville.

To reach the beach in a hurry, get on the
next flight to **Corpus Christi International
Airport** (1000 International Blvd., 361/289-
0171, www.cctexas.com/airport), offering service from American Eagle, Continental, and
Southwest Airlines. South Padre is accessible
via the **Brownsville/South Padre Island
International Airport** (700 S. Minnesota
Ave., 956/542-4373, www.flybrownsville.
com), served by Continental and American
Eagle. Galveston is about an hour-long drive
from Houston. Rental car service is available
at each airport.

Galveston

ocated on an island about 50 miles southeast
f Houston, Galveston (population 56,148)
s a hotbed for Texas history. Most people
remember the Alamo, but they don't realize
Galveston was once Texas's largest city and
busiest port, with thousands of immigrants
arriving each year. Unfortunately, recent hurricanes (2008's Ike, in particular) have been
historic for all the wrong reasons, with devastating winds and waves destroying property
and driving thousands of residents perma-
nently out of town.

Galveston was founded in 1839, and the
island town was emerging as a burgeoning
commercial center until the Civil War put the
brakes on its progress. An interesting historical side note: On January 1, 1863, Confederate
troops recaptured the city, while, on the same
day, Abraham Lincoln signed the final draft of
the Emancipation Proclamation. Word didn't
make it to Galveston until June 19, 1865, when

enslaved Texans officially (finally) received
their freedom. Afterward, Galveston became
the birthplace of the now-national Juneteenth
celebration, which commemorates the June 19
announcement.

After the war, Galveston resumed its steady
growth due to the hundreds of immigrants, primarily German, disembarking from ocean lin-
ers each day. Trade was prosperous, especially
cotton exports, and for a while, Galveston was
known as the "Wall Street of the South" due
to its robust economy and cosmopolitan amenities such as electric lights, telephones, and
modern streetcars.

The stately mansions and downtown business buildings constructed during this era still
stand as the heart of Galveston's historic district. Tourists from across the globe flock to
the island to experience these intricate homes
(most are now history museums) and ornate
commercial architecture.

HIGHLIGHTS

(The Strand: Experience Galveston's
thriving historic district in all its New Orleans-
style splendor, including hotels, restaurants,
art galleries, and boutiques (page 73).

(The _Elissa:_ Get a feel for seafaring life by
walking across the sturdy wooden decks of this
remarkable historic ship, the second-oldest operational sailing vessel in the world (page 77).

(Texas State Aquarium: Visitors experience Texas's Gulf Coast from the ground down
at Corpus Christi's Texas State Aquarium,
starting with birds and gators at sea level and
descending to oil-rig depths with menacing
sharks, a colossal grouper, and hundreds of
other slippery species (page 88).

(USS _Lexington_ Museum: Hop aboard
the massive USS _Lexington_ in the Corpus
Christi Bay, where this decommissioned World
War II naval aircraft carrier transports visitors
back in time with vintage aircraft, tours of its
11 decks, and an impressive collection of historical memorabilia (page 88).

(Padre Island National Seashore:
Not to be confused with its rambunctious little sibling to the south, Padre Island National
Seashore is the longest remaining undeveloped stretch of barrier island in the world
(page 92).

(King Ranch: This 825,000-acre "birthplace of American ranching" evokes the maj-
esty and mystique of Texas culture, from
Longhorn cattle to wide-open spaces to genuine cowboys on a vast expanse of coastal plains
larger than Rhode Island (page 103).

(Port Isabel Lighthouse: It's well worth
the 74-step climb up the lighthouse's tight spiral staircase to experience the breathtaking
views—from the bug-size cars passing over the
gorgeous Laguna Madre Bay to the remarkable
view of historic downtown Port Isbell, the vantage point from this historic lighthouse is truly
a sight to behold (page 109).

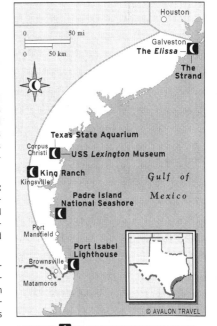

LOOK FOR **(** TO FIND RECOMMENDED SIGHTS,
ACTIVITIES, DINING, AND LODGING.

abundant birding opportunities. The Great
Texas Coastal Birding Trail ties together all
300-plus miles of shoreline, from humming-
birds near Galveston to whooping cranes and
tropical species on Padre Island. Two major migratory flyways intersect along the Gulf Coast,
allowing birders to potentially capture (on a
camera viewfinder) an elusive species on their
"must-see" list.

Though it's hard to imagine why anyone
would want to abandon the recreational opportunities along the shoreline (perhaps your
skin is already too parched), the cool air-
conditioning at numerous Gulf Coast museums
offers a welcome cultural respite. Galveston's
Moody Gardens and several Corpus Christi
attractions are world-class facilities for learning about regional history, wildlife, and art.

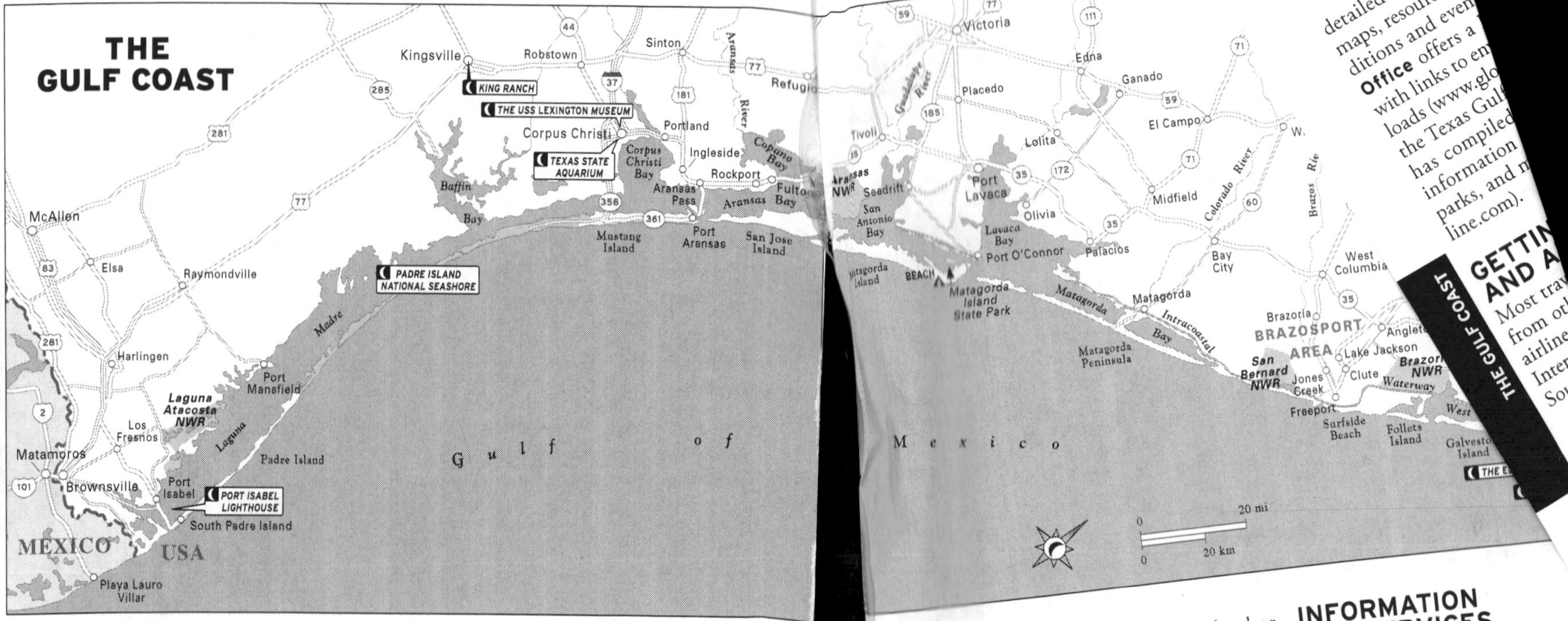

THE GULF COAST

Map labels include: Kingsville, Robstown, Sinton, Victoria, Edna, Ganado, KING RANCH, THE USS LEXINGTON MUSEUM, Corpus Christi, Portland, Refugio, Tivoli, Placedo, El Campo, Lolita, TEXAS STATE AQUARIUM, Corpus Christi Bay, Ingleside, Rockport, Port Lavaca, Midfield, McAllen, Baffin Bay, Aransas Pass, Fulton, Seadrift, Palacios, Bay City, West Columbia, Mustang Island, Port Aransas, San Jose Island, Port O'Connor, Matagorda, Brazoria, BRAZOSPORT AREA, Harlingen, PADRE ISLAND NATIONAL SEASHORE, Matagorda Island State Park, Lake Jackson, Laguna Atacosta NWR, Port Mansfield, Matagorda Peninsula, San Bernard NWR, Jones Creek, Clute, Brazos NWR, Los Fresnos, Matamoros, Padre Island, Gulf of Mexico, Freeport, Surfside Beach, Follets Island, Galveston Island, Brownsville, Port Isabel, PORT ISABEL LIGHTHOUSE, South Padre Island, MEXICO, USA, Playa Lauro Villar

Top your day off with a fresh catch from one of the seaside restaurants for a perfect ending to a Gulf Coast day.

Aside from the festive annual springtime activity in Galveston (Mardi Gras) and South Padre (spring break), most of the Gulf Coast is a year-round, slow-moving vacationland, where the biggest challenge is determining the day's activities—swimming, fishing, shell collecting, sunbathing, surfing, boating, or sand-castle building. Visitors responding to the call of the sea find the region to be as low-key as the gulf's lightly lapping waves.

PLANNING YOUR TIME

Coast-bound travelers tend to stay for a weekend in one area—Galveston, Brazosport, Corpus, or South Padre—to lay claim to a beach condo or hole up in a fishing village as opposed to roaming the entire region. In fact, parking yourself on one beach is the best way to

do it, unless you have time and money to spare and can enjoy your experience cruising along the coast in a boat (rentals are available).

In general, there are two types of Gulf Coast travelers: busy families looking for a getaway from the 'burbs and grizzled fishermen looking for a getaway from the family. The South Padre Island beaches are considered the nicest, so if quality sand and surf are your top priorities, that's the best place to start. Plan to spend at least two to three days soaking up the sun, soft white sand, and gently rolling surf.

As you make your way up the coast, the beaches tend to be less scenic—the sand is a bit darker and the infiltration of civilization is more apparent (oil rigs, trash, tankers, commercial buildings, etc.). Regardless, the scent of salt water and intrinsic lure of the sea are just as strong; you just have to deal with more traffic and city folk. It's worth spending a long weekend in Corpus Christi to soak

up the pleasant scene on Mustang Island or nearby Padre Island National Seashore. The city's USS *Lexington*, Texas State Aquarium, and Museum of Science and History are well worth visiting for a family-friendly, air-conditioned change of pace.

The Brazosport Area offers fewer cultural amenities than its coastal cousins, which is precisely the reason anglers prefer spending quiet weekends here sans water parks and booming car stereos. Things are more low-key and less commercial in this unassuming corner of the coast, where retirees, fishermen, and professional beachcombers peacefully coexist.

Galveston is where the big-city Houston folk go to spend their money and get their beach and seafood fix. It's the least-stunning of all the Gulf Coast beaches, but the waves are still welcoming, and the shopping and restaurant scene in the historic Strand district are certainly deserving of two travel days.

INFORMATION AND SERVICES

Most communities along the Gulf C[...] visitors bureaus where tourists can [...] about directions, equipment rental, and travel-related assistance. Contact the follo[...] entities before your trip with questions ab[...] logistics or scheduling. Physical addresses a[...] hours of operation are included at the end o[...] each destination section in this chapter.

Brazosport Area Chamber of Commerce (979/285-2501, www.brazosport.org), **Corpus Christi Area Convention & Visitors Bureau** (361/881-1800 or 800/766-2322, www.vis-itcorpuschristitx.org), **Galveston Island Convention & Visitors Bureau** (409/763-4311 or 888/425-4753, www.galvestoncvb.com), and **South Padre Island Convention & Visitors Bureau** (956/761-6433 or 800/767-2373, www.sopadre.com).

A couple of helpful websites provide more

Galveston's fate was forever altered in 1900 when a massive hurricane decimated nearly a third of the island's buildings. The torrential 120-mile-per-hour windstorm caused an estimated 6,000 deaths, an inconceivable number of casualties in these 24-hour live-weather radar days. As a result of the devastation, Galveston's industrial and residential populations shifted to Houston.

Galveston eventually recovered from its economically challenging times—thanks in part to the construction of a massive seawall to protect the northern part of the island—to become one of the state's top tourist destinations. Although Hurricane Ike caused widespread damage in 2008 (mainly from flooding), most of the island's cultural and historical attractions survived the storm and have reopened for business. The beach remains the island's main draw, especially for surf-seeking Houstonians, but its rich historic fabric provides a pleasant slice of Victorian-era life for international visitors.

SIGHTS

Most of Galveston's attractions are heritage related, but they're well worth checking out since they're some of the highest-quality cultural sites in the state. The historic commercial buildings along The Strand and the century-old mansions showcase a distinctive and fascinating time in Texas history that visitors won't find throughout the inland regions.

◖ The Strand

The heart of Galveston's thriving business district in the late 1800s and early 1900s, The Strand (Strand and Mechanic Sts. between 20th and 25th Sts.) still captures the essence of the city's "Wall Street of the South" era. This 36-block National Historic Landmark District features New Orleans–style hotels, restaurants, art galleries, and boutiques, most of which escaped the devastation of the 1900 hurricane. Today, visitors flock to the antiques and clothing shops, art studios, and seasonal festivals, including the popular Dickens on the Strand and Mardi Gras celebrations. For information

about recommended shops, lodging options, and eateries throughout The Strand district, consult the corresponding sections in this chapter.

Museums

Most of Galveston's museums are located in historic buildings, offering an ideal opportunity to authentically experience the city's fascinating heritage. The 19th-century house museums, in particular, provide an intimate glimpse into the lives of prominent residents of the time through original furniture, heirlooms, artwork, and informative tours.

BISHOP'S PALACE

Grand. Stately. Ginormous. However you choose to describe it, the spectacular 1886 Bishop's Palace (1402 Broadway St., 409/762-2475, www.galvestonhistory.org, Mon.–Sat. 11 A.M.–4 P.M., Sun. noon–4 P.M., guided tours every hour, $10 adults, $7 students) is the centerpiece of Galveston's historic Broadway

Bishop's Palace

Street. The American Institute of Architects designated Bishop's Palace as one of the 100 outstanding buildings in the country, and it's easy to see why. This Victorian castle exudes elegance, from its ornate fireplaces (one is lined with pure silver) to its grand stairway to its stained-glass windows and intricately carved furnishings and details. The Bishop's Palace is Galveston's most visited historical attraction for good reason—its stately design and detailed furnishings transport visitors to another era, offering an escape to the past unmatched in this part of the country.

MOODY MANSION

Nearly as impressive in its opulence is the nearby Moody Mansion (2618 Broadway St., 409/762-7668, www.moodymansion. org, daily 11 A.M.–3 P.M., tours held on the hour 10 A.M.–3 P.M., $7 adults, $3.50 students). Renowned Galveston entrepreneur and businessman W. L. Moody Jr. purchased the four-story, 32-room, 28,000-square-foot limestone and brick mansion a week after the 1900 hurricane. The stately home features rare hand-carved wood, coffered ceilings, stained glass, and heirlooms from the Moody family, who established one of the country's most heralded financial empires through various entrepreneurial endeavors (cotton, banking, ranching, and insurance). Marvel at the manicured grounds, exquisite furnishings, the expansive ballroom, and the dining room's gold-leaf ceiling.

ASHTON VILLA

Also of interest to history enthusiasts is the remarkable 1859 Ashton Villa (2328 Broadway St., 409/762-3933, www.galvestonhistory. org, call in advance about hours of operation, tours, and admission fees). This stately mansion, built for one of Texas's wealthiest businessmen, James Moreau Brown, set the standard for the exquisite Galveston homes that followed. Experience the Victorian lifestyle through the home's grand entryway, life-size paintings, and beautifully landscaped grounds. The house contains many pieces of

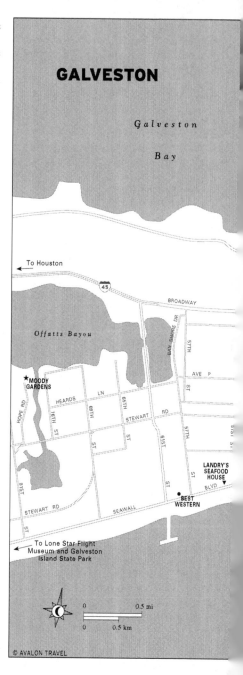

THE GULF COAST

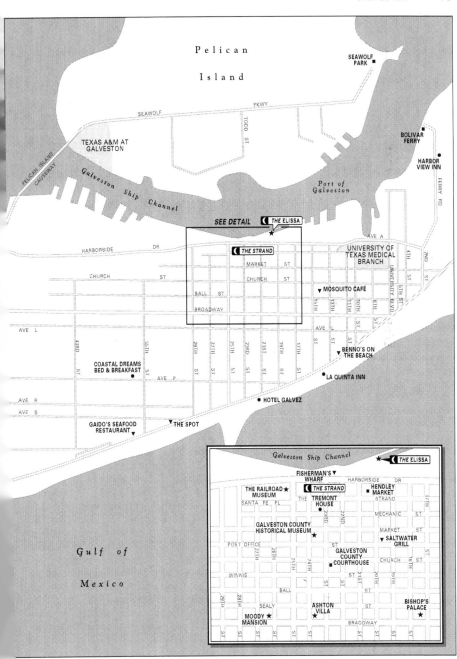

Pelican Island

SEAWOLF PARK

PKWY

SEAWOLF

TODD ST

TEXAS A&M AT GALVESTON

BOLIVAR FERRY

HARBOR VIEW INN

FERRY RD

Galveston Ship Channel

Port of Galveston

SEE DETAIL THE ELISSA

HARBORSIDE DR

AVE A

THE STRAND

MARKET ST

CHURCH ST

UNIVERSITY OF TEXAS MEDICAL BRANCH

UNIVERSITY BLVD

CHURCH ST

BALL ST

▼ MOSQUITO CAFÉ

BROADWAY

25TH 13TH 11TH 10TH 8TH ST

4TH 2ND

5TH ST

AVE L

43RD 35TH 29TH 27TH 25TH 23RD 21ST 19TH 17TH ST

AVE L

COASTAL DREAMS BED & BREAKFAST ●

AVE P

ST

BENNO'S ON THE BEACH ▼

● LA QUINTA INN

AVE R

AVE S

● HOTEL GALVEZ

GAIDO'S SEAFOOD RESTAURANT ▼

▼ THE SPOT

Gulf of

Mexico

Galveston Ship Channel

 THE ELISSA

FISHERMAN'S WHARF ▼

HARBORSIDE DR

THE RAILROAD MUSEUM ★

HENDLEY MARKET ■

 THE STRAND

SANTA FE PL

THE TREMONT HOUSE ●

STRAND

MECHANIC ST

17TH

GALVESTON COUNTY HISTORICAL MUSEUM ★

23RD 22ND

MARKET ST

▼ SALTWATER GRILL

POST OFFICE

27TH 26TH 25TH 24TH

ST

GALVESTON COUNTY COURTHOUSE ■

CHURCH ST

16TH ST

21ST 20TH

WINNIE

BALL ST

ST

29TH 28TH

SEALY

ASHTON VILLA ★

BISHOP'S PALACE ★

MOODY MANSION ★

BROADWAY

ST

Moody Mansion

artwork, furniture, and mementos the family acquired during its travels to the Far East. Ashton Villa now houses the city's Heritage Visitors Center, which is open daily, but, as of early 2011, tours of the mansion are still on hold as Hurricane Ike–related work continues on its interior.

LONE STAR FLIGHT MUSEUM
Located on the island's west end, the Lone Star Flight Museum (2002 Terminal Dr., 409/740-7722, www.lsfm.org, daily 9 a.m.–5 p.m., $8 adults, $5 seniors and students) features an impressive collection of vintage warbirds, including a rare operational SBD Dauntless, a AT-6/SNJ Texan trainer, and a mighty B-17 Flying Fortress. Children will marvel at the vintage planes that carried bombs and fought enemies from the sky, and their parents (or grandparents) are welcome to experience the planes authentically from the cockpit as part of the museum's flight program. Most of the airplanes are operational, and the flights (with a trained pilot) are a once-in-a-lifetime experience for

the World War II buff in your family. Check the website for pricing and details.

THE RAILROAD MUSEUM
Anchoring Galveston's historic downtown Strand district is the former Santa Fe Union Station, home to The Railroad Museum (2602 Santa Fe Pl., 409/765-5700, www.galveston-rrmuseum.com, call ahead regarding hours of operation and admission). More than 20,000 railroad items and several dozen vintage passenger, dining, and kitchen cars provide fascinating views of railroad life from the late 19th and early 20th centuries. The main terminal, located at the heart of this impressive art deco building, contains interactive exhibits and a collection of unique plaster sculptures depicting "ghosts of travelers past." Kids will love the miniature model trains and the historic rail cars behind the passenger depot. Note: The museum suffered damage from Hurricane Ike and remained under construction in early 2011—visitors should call ahead to determine accessibility.

GALVESTON COUNTY HISTORICAL MUSEUM

The best way to get a full appreciation of Galveston's past is at its remarkable downtown history museum (2219 Market St., 409/766-2340, www.co.galveston.tx.us, call regarding hours of operation). Housed inside the spectacular 1921 City National Bank building, the museum contains more than a dozen exhibits showcasing the region's history, all beneath a remarkably ornate barreled ceiling. Learn about the Native Americans, European explorers, and Civil War battles that shaped Galveston Island, and be sure to look for a small television screen offering an extremely rare view of the havoc caused by the 1900 hurricane. Known simply as the "Edison video," this grainy black-and-white archival movie footage was commissioned by Thomas Edison to use his new invention, the "motion picture camera." The rough images show ravaged boats and docks, bringing to life the utter destruction that befell the island. Note: As of early 2011, the museum was still "temporarily" closed due to damage from Hurricane Ike—visitors should call ahead to determine accessibility.

◖ The *Elissa*

One of the city's most treasured landmarks is the 1877 ship *Elissa* (Pier 21, 409/763-1877, www.tsm-elissa.org, 10 A.M.–5 P.M. daily, $8 adults, $5 students ages 6 and up). This remarkable historic ship is the second-oldest operational sailing vessel in the world and one of the three oldest merchant boats still afloat. Get a feel for seafaring life by walking across the sturdy wooden decks under massive masts and 19 sails, and exploring the sleeping quarters and mechanical room. While below deck, be sure to take a few minutes to view the professional documentary about the boat's dramatic shipyard rescue. Incidentally, the *Elissa* was one of the few historical attractions in Galveston that was largely unharmed by Hurricane Ike, losing only a few sails while remaining anchored to the seafloor. For those interested, the ship has been designated an

the *Elissa*

American Treasure by the National Trust for Historic Preservation.

To learn more about *Elissa*'s history and subsequent restoration, visit the adjacent **Texas Seaport Museum.** The portside facility features informative exhibits about maritime culture, a fascinating movie about Galveston's port-based heritage as the "Ellis Island of the West," and a computer database with the names of more than 133,000 immigrants who entered the United States through Galveston.

Moody Gardens

Natural wonders await beneath three enormous glass pyramids at Moody Gardens (1 Hope Blvd., 409/744-4673, www.moodygardens.com, daily 10 A.M.–6 P.M., $40 for a one-day pass, $10 average for individual attractions). One of Galveston's most popular and prominent attractions, Moody Gardens offers an elaborate and stunning collection of plants, animals, and educational exhibits inside its colossal 100-foot-tall structures. The all-access day pass carries a hefty price tag, so if

HURRICANES: DEADLY TROPICAL CYCLONES

Hurricane season is a tumultuous time for Gulf Coast residents. These devastating tropical cyclones can come ashore anytime between June and November, though most strike in the hot summer months of August and September.

Hurricanes originate when ocean waters reach their highest temperatures, leading to thunderstorms with winds of up to 40 miles per hour (officially a tropical storm). At this point, the National Hurricane Center names the storm, working from a predetermined alphabetical list of names. Tropical storms get their energy from warm, humid air over the ocean, and the release of this force is what drives the powerful winds of a hurricane.

Traditionally, the probability of a hurricane hitting Texas hasn't been too severe, but the past few years have been a different story. In September 2005, Hurricane Rita, a Category 5 storm with intense 120-mph winds, made landfall near Sabine Pass on the Texas-Louisiana border. It ultimately caused more than $11 billion in damage and is linked to seven deaths. Even more devastating size wise was Hurricane Ike, which slammed into Galveston Island in September 2008, leaving an enormous swath of destruction in its wake. Ike completely leveled several nearby communities, and its 110-mph winds ripped apart hotels, office buildings, and countless homes in Galveston, Houston, and the surrounding area.

In general, however, the statistical possibility of Texas being hit by a hurricane is not too severe (one every six years along any 50-mile segment of the Texas coast). The recent experiences, plus the fresh memory of 2005's devastating Hurricane Katrina in New Orleans, is serious enough to make residents tune in to the weather radar every time the words *tropical depression* surface. More often than not, the storm bypasses the gulf or dissipates by the time it reaches the Texas coast. According to weather researchers, annual probabilities of a hurricane striking a 50-mile segment of the coast range from roughly 30 percent near Port Arthur to nearly 40 percent at Matagorda Bay northeast of Corpus Christi.

That being said, some of the strongest hurricanes to hit the U.S. coast have come ashore in Texas. Unlike the overwhelmingly destructive effects of Hurricane Ike in Galveston, however, the storms that historically ravaged Texas are typically in uninhabited areas. In 1970, meteorologists recorded wind gusts of 180 miles per hour near Aransas Pass, and in 1961, Hurricane Carla brought 175-mph winds to Port Lavaca. By comparison, Katrina's wind speeds were 140 miles per hour at landfall, but its extremely low barometric pressure made it improbably intense.

In the wake of the devastating losses associated with Hurricane Ike, Texas officials have organized emergency plans and evacuation routes for coastal cities. Public awareness campaigns focus on the importance of being informed and prepared. The unpredictable nature of these storms makes evacuation planning a challenge, but an increasing number of Gulf Coast residents are erring on the safe side when an intensifying tropical storm is on the horizon by packing up and moving inland until the tempest subsides.

---

you'd rather choose just one area to explore, go with the Rainforest Pyramid. The Aquarium Pyramid has more animals and features, but the Rainforest environment is a unique experience, where you'll find yourself face-to-face with African jungle animals, tropical birds, and colorful reptiles. Massive plants, cascading waterfalls, and the constant chatter of birds and insects transport you across the planet to these exotic habitats. Be sure to check out the bat cave, with various species of bats hanging upside-down, nibbling on fresh fruit.

The Aquarium Pyramid takes you on a journey across the world's oceans, viewed at two levels—surface and underwater. Marvel at penguins as they waddle and dive, and catch an up-close view of sea lions as they glide and play. Sharks, sea turtles, rays, and tropical fish await below the surface, viewable in a traditional aquarium tank setting or from the underwater tunnel surrounded by one million gallons of water.

Other notable attractions include the Discovery Pyramid, featuring science and nature exhibits; three IMAX "ridefilm" theaters; kids' activities aboard the *Colonel* Paddlewheel Boat; seasonal recreation at Palm Beach (swimming lagoons, whirlpools, volleyball, and paddleboats); formal gardens; nature trails; and the esteemed Moody Gardens conference center, hotel, and spa.

SHOPPING

Shopping is one of Galveston's main draws, with abundant fashion boutiques and knick-knack shops throughout the historic downtown area. Keep in mind, this is where wealthy Houstonians come to play, so items are often priced for this clientele.

The Strand

The gas-lit street lamps, ornate architectural detailing, and lofty display windows along the 36-block Strand district even attract nonshoppers with their Victorian-era charm. One of the first places many people start their browsing is the eclectic **Hendley Market** (2010 Strand St., 409/762-2610, www.hendleymarket.com). This fascinating emporium contains a little bit of everything, from Mexican imports to vintage jewelry to kitschy knick-knacks to antique medical instruments. Kids will love the baskets filled with hand-crafted toys and plastic novelty trinkets. Not quite as charming yet equally beguiling with its amazing array of objects is **Big House Antiques** (2212 Mechanic St., 409/762-0559). Shoppers will find many estate-sale pieces here, including furniture, jewelry, decorative items, and books. For a modest increase on the price and quality scale, step into the **Front Parlor** (2111 Strand St., 409/762-0224, www.thefrontparlor.com), where the sign out front promises Books, Gifts, and Surprises. Though the store specializes in fancy Lampe Berger lamps imported from Paris, the Front Parlor also features home accessories and women's clothing.

This being Texas, shoppers may want to mosey through **Way Out West** (2317 Strand St., 409/766-7837). Like most Western-themed gift shops, some of the items here get a bit hokey (garish Lone Star State posters and T-shirts), but for the most part, Way Out West offers tasteful gifts, including silver jewelry, home decor objects, wind chimes, and hand-carved woodwork.

If you forgot your flip-flops or lost your sunglasses on the beach, drop by the **Jammin Sportswear** (2314 Strand St., 409/763-4005). Every beach town needs a few good T-shirt shops, and Jammin Sportswear is one of the most popular on the island. Pick up towels, caps, sunscreen, or even one of those bitey alligator toys here. A step up is **Surf Styles** (2119 Strand St., 409/763-0147), where you can get a T-shirt for the beach and some stylish cruisewear for a night on the town. Brands include Stussy, Miss Me Denim, Converse, and Lucky Brand.

A mandatory stop on The Strand is the venerable **Old Strand Emporium** (2112 Strand St., 409/515-0715). The longest-running spot in the district, the Old Strand Emporium offers fresh fudge, ice cream, deli sandwiches, and cold drinks, including beers and wine. Texas foods are the specialty here, so be sure to grab a jar of salsa, a pecan praline, or some tangy barbecue sauce.

ACCOMMODATIONS

Galveston's popularity as a tourist destination means there's no shortage of lodging options. From cheap beachside motels to luxurious resorts, the island has something for everyone.

Seawall Boulevard

For most visitors, the best way to experience an island vacation is on the shoreline. Though the following selection of hotels aren't technically on the beach—you'll have to cross busy Seawall Boulevard to get your toes in the sand—they're close enough to smell the salty air and see the sailboats and barges.

At the affordable end of the scale is the

no-frills yet dependable **Gaido's Seaside Inn** (3700 Seawall Blvd., 409/762-9625, www. gaidosofgalveston.com, $79 d). Gaido's is perhaps best known for its incredible adjacent seafood restaurant, but the hotel has some tasty amenities, too, including a free continental breakfast, an outdoor pool, and free coffee and juice in the lobby. Another well-regarded local establishment is the nearby **Commodore on the Beach** (3618 Seawall Blvd., 409/763-2375, www.commodoreonthebeach.com, $109 d). The Commodore features rooms with balconies facing the beach, a large pool with a welcoming cascading fountain, and several complimentary services, including wireless Internet access, continental breakfast, coffee and juice, and late-afternoon cookies.

Some travelers value the comfort and familiarity of chain hotels, and, although the corporate options are nearly outnumbered by independent establishments on Seawall, there are several offering competitive rates and reliable service. Among them is **La Quinta East Beach** (1402 Seawall Blvd., 409/763-1224, www.lq.com, $64 d), featuring an outdoor pool along with a free continental breakfast and Internet access. Though the accommodations aren't luxurious, there's something very appealing about the comfy beach-town vibe here and especially the ocean view (and smell) directly outside your hotel room door. Another option farther down the island is the more expensive and fancier **Best Western Beach Front Inn** (5914 Seawall Blvd., 409/740-1261, www.bestwesterngalveston.com, $159 d), offering a free continental breakfast, Internet access, and free cappuccino and hot chocolate. The Best Western also claims to have the only heated pool on the island.

Those willing to drop some extra cash for a truly memorable vacation experience should consider the remarkable **C Hotel Galvez** (2024 Seawall Blvd., 409/765-7721, www. wyndham.com, $197 d). Known as the "Queen of the Gulf" when it opened in 1911, the Galvez is stunning in its Victorian elegance. Luxurious amenities include a pool with swim-up bar,

marble bathrooms, wireless Internet access, and an impressive spa and workout facility. Not nearly as historic yet similarly stylish is the **Galveston Island Hilton** (5400 Seawall Blvd., 409/744-5000, www.galvestonhilton. com, $295 d), featuring large rooms with plush robes, Wi-Fi service, gulf view rooms with private balconies, a tropically landscaped pool, and a fitness center.

Strand Area

If you'd rather be within walking distance of shopping than seashells, make reservations at the exquisite **C Tremont House** (2300 Ship's Mechanic Row, 409/763-0300, www.wyndham.com, $179 d). Located in the heart of The Strand historic commercial district, the Tremont is a stunning 1879 Victorian hotel that transports guests to Galveston's heyday as the "Wall Street of the South." The first things you'll notice in the rooms are the lofty ceilings and incredibly tall windows. Wrought-iron beds, marble bathrooms, antique furnishings, and a stylish black-and-white color scheme add to the elegant environment. Modern touches include free wireless Internet access and Web TV. Just down the street is the **Harbor House** (28 Pier #21, 409/763-3321, www.harborhousepier21.com, $195 d), which is fancy in a completely different way. It's not historic, but the Harbor House offers an amazing vantage point of the busy harbor and bustling marina activity. One of the best seafood restaurants in town (Willie G's) is across the street, and the hotel provides free passes to a nearby fitness center. Amenities include wireless Internet access and a free continental breakfast.

Bed-and-Breakfasts

With so many impressive historic structures in a pedestrian-friendly vacation environment, Galveston is an ideal place to stay in a B&B. One of the more popular options is **The Inn at 1816 Postoffice** (1816 Post Office St., 888/558-9444, www.inn1816postoffice. com, weekend rates start at $159), located in the heart of the East End Historic District. This 1886 Victorian home is an elegant sight to behold, and its amenities are equally impressive, including wireless Internet access, a game room with a pool table and board games, bikes for an island cruise or trip to the beach, and packed picnic baskets (for a small fee). Another commendable option is **Avenue O Bed and Breakfast** (2323 Ave. O, 409/762-2868, www.avenueo.com, rooms start at $99), just a few blocks away from the beach. This 1923 Mediterranean-style home sits on a sizable piece of property surrounded by tropical foliage. Breakfasts are hearty here, and snacks are available throughout the day. Avenue O also provides bikes for island excursions. Just down the street is **Coastal Dreams Bed & Breakfast** (3602 Ave. P, 409/770-0270, www.coastaldreamsbnb.com, rooms start at $139). Built in 1887, this remarkable home boasts 12-foot ceilings and stained-glass windows, and an inviting pool. Breakfasts feature stuffed French toast, thick bacon slices, and omelets, and daytime treats include fresh baked cookies, brownies, and other sweets.

Camping

If you prefer lodging in an RV or tent, you'll enjoy **Galveston Island State Park** (14901 FM 3005, 409/737-1222, www.tpwd.state.tx.us, daily entry fee $5 per person ages 13 and older, camping fees $15–25 per night). Though portions of the park were damaged by Hurricane Ike, most of the campsites and facilities have reopened. Located on the west end of Galveston Island about 10 miles from town, Galveston Island State Park offers 2,000 acres of natural beauty along the Gulf Coast. Even if you aren't planning to spend the night, the park is a great place for swimming, hiking, birdwatching, and mountain biking. Educational tours of the coastline's native plants and animals are available by appointment—contact the park to make arrangements. Expect to encounter and learn about trout, redfish, croaker, and flounder as well as tropical birds, ducks, marsh rabbits, and armadillos.

Park facilities include four miles of hike and bike trails, an interpretive center and nature trail, concrete boat ramp, fish-cleaning shelter, campsites with water and electricity, screened camping shelters, restrooms with showers, outdoor showers, picnic sites, and Wi-Fi access. The park contains 140 campsites with electricity and water hookups, and 10 screened shelters.

Less scenic yet more centrally located is the **Bayou Shores RV Resort** (6310 Heards Ln., 409/744-2837). Located just off the causeway, the RV park offers standard hookups as well as a fishing pier and exercise facility.

FOOD

There's no excuse to not eat seafood in Galveston; fortunately, the city is brimming with quality restaurants, and almost all of them survived Hurricane Ike. After you've had your fill of shrimp, oysters, and snapper, try some of the Southern-style comfort food at one of the island's tremendous neighborhood joints.

Downtown
AMERICAN
The Strand is filled with confectioners' shops and small eateries that come and go, but several have become mainstays for lunch breaks during prolonged bouts of shopping. Among them is the aptly named **Lunchbox Cafe** (213 23rd St., 409/770-0044, www.thelunchboxcafegalveston, $6–18), a family-friendly spot with character that specializes in healthy sandwiches and salads. Sandwiches are a step beyond expectations, with nice touches like fresh organic apple slices on the turkey and Brie. The Cape Cod salad is also excellent, with a flavorful blend of field greens.

Step back in time at the charming and moderately priced **Star Drug Store** (510 23rd St., 409/766-7719, www.galvestondrug.com, $5–10). The historic neon/porcelain Coca-Cola sign out front sets the tone for this establishment, featuring an ancient (well, more than a century old) horseshoe-shaped lunch counter with soda fountain. Not surprisingly, the menu options are typical old-time lunch fare: burgers, Reubens, pimiento cheese sandwiches, chicken salad, dilled pasta salad, and ice-cream floats. The drugstore's signature item is a tasty tomato-basil soup.

SEAFOOD

What else are you going to eat in Galveston? Put aside your craving for Mongolian or Canadian cuisine for a few days and savor the local flavor. Fresh seafood is everywhere in Galveston, and several of the best places are right on the bay just a few blocks from The Strand district.

There's something about arriving in a seaside town that creates an instant yearning for enjoying a plate of shrimp or oyster or snapper—sometimes all three—while overlooking the water. If you're in the downtown area, satisfy this urge at the low-key yet high-quality **Willie G's** (2100 Harborside, 409/762-3030, www.williegs.com, $9–31). Opt for bayside seating and let your ocean vacation begin. Order some peel-and-eat shrimp to start—squeeze fresh lemon on top and dip them in tangy cocktail sauce—and proceed to the fresh catch of the day, from blackened snapper to grilled flounder to fried trout. Welcome to Galveston! Next door is the larger and consistently dependable **Fisherman's Wharf** (Pier 22 and Harborside Dr., 409/765-5708, $9–30). Red snapper is the specialty here, but feel free to cast your eyes and teeth at everything on the menu—shrimp kisses, oysters on the half shell, calamari, and even the steak and pasta are all tempting and tasty. Be sure to ask for a table with a view of the bay, where you can sit on the deck and watch the shrimp boats slowly glide by.

About a half mile inland you'll find one of the finest (and most expensive) restaurants in town. The fabulous **(Saltwater Grill** (2017 Post Office St., 409/762-3474, $12–42) feels urban and spare like Houston but tastes fresh and flavorful like a Gulf Coast restaurant should. At Saltwater, *fresh* isn't just an appealing adjective, it's a genuine approach to food preparation. The restaurant utilizes a bizarre yet effective steam-kettle device that's linked to a large heater, pipes, and steel buckets that cause water to boil in merely three minutes. The result is rapidly cooked fresh seafood as opposed to reheated or perpetually boiling (and soaking) fare. Enjoy the results on a plate of mussels, clams, or shrimp, and be sure to order

the grand gumbo. Another must-taste is the appetizer dish with fried asparagus topped with crabmeat and entrées such as the grilled yellowfin tuna, red snapper, and seafood linguini. It's worth dropping by the next day for a big bowl of gumbo. Reservations are recommended.

Seawall and Vicinity
AMERICAN

One of the best restaurants in the entire region is just a few minutes from the shore at **(Mosquito Café** (628 14th St., 409/763-1010, www.mosquitocafe.com, $6–19, open at 11 A.M. Tues–Fri., 8 A.M. on weekends). You'll definitely want to have breakfast here at least once, and you may find yourself returning for each meal since the flavor-packed, creatively inspired, healthy food makes such an impression. Grab a hot mug of strong coffee and try to decide among the delectable options such as Mosquito Benedict (a fresh-baked scone covered with portabello mushrooms, sautéed shrimp, sun-dried tomatoes, artichoke hearts, asparagus, and poached eggs topped with serrano hollandaise sauce), cinnamon-tinged French toast, fluffy pancakes, or bagels and lox. Lunch items include hearty bowls of pasta with homemade pesto, olives, and feta cheese, or tasty sandwiches on delicious fresh-baked bread with hickory-smoked bacon, avocado salsa, and goat cheese.

For a simple, low-key breakfast, lunch, or dinner, drop by the nearby neighborhood stalwart **Sunflower Bakery and Cafe** (512 14th St., 409/763-5500, $4–10, closed Sun.). You'll find warm, soft, fresh-made bakery items (breads, pastries, desserts) and flavor-packed sandwiches (the turkey, bacon, and avocado on honey wheat bread is especially tasty) along with healthy salads and even a few eclectic daily specials. Along with its newer (and less charming) location in a retail center, the Sunflower has expanded its options, offering a fresh and full menu complete with crab cakes, burgers, and po'boys. Incidentally, this is the perfect place to order a to-go lunch for the beach—just don't forget to include brownies and their legendary strawberry lemonade.

SEAFOOD

If you're staying in a hotel on Seawall Boulevard, your inaugural meal should definitely be at **Gaido's Seafood Restaurant** (3800 Seawall Blvd., 409/762-9625, $8–29). This venerable institution has been serving memorable meals since 1911, and its legendary reputation is evident everywhere, from the time-honored trimmings to the traditional menu to attentive service. The shrimp bisque is exquisite, the garlic snapper is succulent, and the crab cakes are outstanding.

For an amazing lunch with an outstanding view you gotta hit **The Spot** (3204 Seawall Blvd., 409/621-5237, www.thespotgalveston. com, $8–19). After a morning or afternoon of beachcombing, this is a spot-on place for a shrimp po'boy, fish-and-chips, or even a big ol' burger. The breading and bread are what set this spot aside from others, with their perfectly crispy texture encasing fresh-flavored seafood and top-notch sandwiches. A big bonus: The second-floor deck offers panoramic views of the gulf almost as tasty as the food in front of you.

Although it's a regional chain, **Landry's Seafood House** (5310 Seawall Blvd., 409/744-1010, www.landrysseafoodhouse.com, $6–27) is a respected eatery, even in a Gulf Coast town known for its local legends. Opt for the fresh catch Lafitte, gulf red snapper, or broiled flounder. Landry's also does shrimp well, including a fried option stuffed with seafood.

Specializing in the Cajun variety of seafood is **Benno's on the Beach** (1200 Seawall Blvd., 409/762-4621, www.bennosofgalveston.com). This is a very unassuming place—guests order at the counter beneath dim fluorescent lights

JELLYFISH JAM

The "jellies" on Texas's Gulf Coast aren't tasty fruit-filled breakfast treats. They're jellyfish, and despite their iridescent and wiggly appearance, they'll cause much more pain than pleasure.

One of the most common creatures washed up on the shore isn't technically a jellyfish, despite its translucent air bubble and blue tentacles. The Portuguese man-of-war (aka the bluebubble, bluebottom, or man-of-war) is actually a colony of organisms, each with its own distinct function. Its name comes from the air bubble's resemblance to the sails of an ancient Portuguese war vessel.

The man-of-war floats on ocean currents and is deposited ashore on Texas beaches during the spring to late summer. These crafty carnivores feed on small fish and other small animals that get caught in their venom-filled tentacles. The other washed-up organisms visitors may encounter on the shoreline are traditional jellyfish – gelatinous invertebrates with varying-size tentacles hanging from the main "body" of the organism (technically referred to as the mollusk).

You won't find an abundance of these bizarre animals on a typical beach stroll, but it's worth keeping an eye out for them because their stings pack quite a wallop. They're much harder to see in the water, but a good indication of their presence is the appearance of any washed-up organisms on the beach. The man-of-war is especially difficult to see since it's translucent and often blends in with wave foam.

Aside from avoiding areas of the ocean where you see beached jellies, you'll have to make sure you don't step anywhere near the washed-up variety, since their stinging cells remain toxic even when the rest of the body has died. Often, the tentacles are nearly invisible, though you'll definitely feel the sharp shot of pain jetting up your leg.

If this happens, scrape the tentacles off with a driver's license or credit card. If you're stung by a jellyfish, place the affected area under hot water and apply hydrocortisone cream to relieve the itching. For a man-of-war sting, splash the area with saltwater, then apply vinegar or a diluted bleach solution (1 part bleach to 10 parts water) to the sting site without pressing too hard on the skin. The pain should go away within an hour.

and sit on hard plastic booth chairs, but as soon as the food arrives, it's apparent where Benno's focuses its resources. The shrimp dishes are spectacular, bursting with flavor and perfectly seasoned with Cajun spices. You also can't go wrong with Benno's crawfish étouffée, jambalaya, spicy crab, or oysters.

RECREATION
Beaches

There are two main beaches in Galveston: the mellow family beach and the raucous singles beach. Both serve important purposes, but it's probably best they're separated. The family-friendly spot is **Stewart Beach** (6th St. and Seawall Blvd., 409/765-5023, $8 admission per car—cash only, open Mar.–mid-Oct.), where you'll find moms, dads, and kids building sand castles, playing volleyball, and body surfing. Nearby amenities include a children's playground with water slides, umbrella and chair rentals, concession area, souvenir shop, restrooms, and a bathhouse. Things get a bit crazier at **East Beach** (1923 Boddeker Dr., 409/762-3278, $8 admission per car—cash only). This is where Houston's younger crowd comes to party, a rare surfside treat since East Beach is one of the few places where drinking is legal on the beach. As a result, you'll find more concerts, promotions, and festivals than other public stretches of shoreline. Up to 7,000 cars can pack the beach (parking and drinking/sunbathing is a popular activity), and the bar area is a magnet for partygoers. East Beach also includes restrooms with showers, volleyball courts, chair and umbrella rentals, and a souvenir shop.

INFORMATION AND SERVICES

The **Galveston Convention and Visitors Bureau** offers brochures and maps with friendly staff on hand to answer questions. Visit the CVB at 523 24th Street or call 866/505-4456. You can also visit their information-packed and user-friendly website at www.galvestoncvb.com. Contact the **Galveston Historical Foundation** at 502 20th Street

(409/765-7834, www.galvestonhistory.org) for information about the island's impressive historic attractions.

GETTING THERE AND AROUND

The island's unique public transportation service, **Galveston Island Trolley** (409/797-3900, www.islandtransit.net, $1.25 adults), was damaged in Hurricane Ike but plans to be back on the rails soon. Call ahead to determine if it is offering similar services to its pre-Ike days: transportation from the Seawall to The Strand district and Pier 21. The cars are charming replicas of those used in Galveston from the late 1800s to the 1930s.

BRAZOSPORT AREA

Brazosport isn't a town name, but a collection of eight Brazoria County communities southwest of Galveston offering a strange mix of lightly developed beachfront and petrochemical plants. For the record, the Brazosport communities are: Clute, Freeport, Jones Creek, Lake Jackson, Oyster Creek, Quintana Beach, Richwood, and Surfside Beach.

The area is rich in Texas history, with the state's earliest explorers landing on nearby beaches nearly 500 years ago and Stephen F. Austin's first colony settling along the rich bottomlands of the Brazos, Colorado, and San Bernard Rivers in the early 19th century. The venerable Texas term Old Three Hundred refers to the 300 settlers who received land grants for Austin's first colony, where each family received up to 4,000 acres of fertile farm and ranch property in the area.

The massive Gulf Intracoastal Waterway carves a path along the coastal lowlands. This commercial boating canal, constructed in the 1940s, is considered the most valuable waterway in the country, transporting as much tonnage annually as the Panama Canal. The protected waterway stretches more than 1,000 miles from Brownsville to Florida.

Visitors to the Brazosport region enjoy the small-town specialty and antiques shops, beach home rentals, and casual ocean-based recreation. Drive, walk, or swim along the 21-mile stretch of beach or watch the seagulls and ocean barges lazily glide by. Other popular recreational activities include fresh- and saltwater fishing, boating, crabbing, and surfing.

Sights and Recreation

A must-see attraction in the Brazosport Area is the spectacular **《 Sea Center Texas** (300 Medical Dr. in Lake Jackson, 979/292-0100, www.tpwd.state.tx.us, Tues.–Sat. 9 A.M.–4 P.M., Sun. 1–4 P.M., free admission). Sea Center Texas is a multiuse facility combining several aquariums, an education center, and a fish hatchery along with an outdoor wetland exhibit and a kids' fishing pond. The education center's main exhibit is a 50,000-gallon aquarium containing Gulf of Mexico marine animals such as nurse sharks, Atlantic spadefish, red drum, gray snapper, and an enormous moray eel. Other large aquariums house tropical species found in area slat marshes, coastal bays, jetties, and artificial and coral reefs. Kids will love the center's "touch pool," where they can gently handle marine animals such as several varieties of crabs, snails, and anemones. Outside, the wetland exhibit is accessible by a long boardwalk over several marsh areas. Families can bring along a nature checklist and activity book to identify species in the area, including green tree frogs, turtles, and a wide variety of birds. The adjacent hatchery has the capacity to produce 20 million fingerlings each year (mostly spotted sea trout and red drum) for release into Texas coastal waters. Tours are available by reservation only.

Regional culture converges at the **The Center for the Arts & Sciences** (400 College Blvd. in Clute, 979/265-7661, www.bcfas.org, Tues.–Sat. 10 A.M.–4 P.M., Sun. 2–5 P.M., free admission). This all-inclusive facility is home to the Brazosport Art League, the Brazosport Museum of Natural Science, the Center Stages Theater, and Brazosport Planetarium. With so many cultural activities sharing space under one roof, you'll find an amazing array of attractions, from a colossal collection of seashells to an art gallery and studio to a theater

staging regional productions. Perhaps most impressive is the natural science museum, containing wildlife, fossils, and an aquarium. Be sure to check out the exhibit featuring the Lightening Whelk (Texas's state shell) and the planetarium, which offers public viewings and occasionally serves as a training facility for astronauts from NASA's nearby Johnson Space Center.

Beaches
SURFSIDE BEACH

If you don't mind a petrochemical plant as your scenic backdrop, Surfside Beach is a delightful getaway for some low-key recreational activity. Though most of the folks here are Houston residents looking for a respite from the Galveston crowds, you'll find other beach lovers here from across the state seeking similar solace. Popular Surfside Beach pastimes include fishing, swimming, sailing, camping, and shell collecting. For information about the village of Surfside Beach, including restaurants, shops, and lodging links, visit www.surfsidebeachtx.org or call 979/233-1531.

BRYAN BEACH

Just a few miles away near the community of Freeport is Bryan Beach, another casual, scenic stretch of surf and sand. Grab a bucket for some sand dollar collecting, a pole for shallow surf fishing, or a towel and sunscreen for sunbathing. Primitive campsites are available nearby. To reach the beach from Freeport, travel two miles southwest of town on FM 1495, then head three miles south on Gulf Beach Road.

Brazoria National Wildlife Refuge

This sizable wildlife refuge (24907 FM 2004 in Angleton, 979/964-4011, www.fws.gov) contains protected habitats offering safe harbor for animals, particularly birds. Its prime location on the Gulf Coast draws more than 200 bird species, one of the highest counts in the nation. In winter, more than 100,000 snow geese, Canadian geese, teal, ducks, and sandhill cranes fill the numerous ponds and sloughs. In summer you'll find herons, egrets, white ibis, spoonbills, seaside sparrows, and scissor-tailed flycatchers. Alligators occupy the refuge year-round on Big Slough and in ponds. Look for their trails thorough the mud and "gator holes" in dryer months.

San Bernard National Wildlife Refuge

The other major refuge in the Brazosport area is San Bernard (6801 County Rd. 306 in Brazoria, 979/849-6062, www.fws.gov). This 24,000-acre protected area is a haven for snow geese, warblers, herons, egrets, ibis, gulls, and terns. Most of the refuge is closed to the public, but the accessible three-mile car tour and several miles of hiking trails offer access to high-quality wildlife viewing.

Fishing

The Brazosport area offers a multitude of facilities for fishing, either inshore or deep-sea. If you choose to keep your feet on the ground, there are plenty of jetties, piers, and beaches where you can cast a line for speckled trout, flounder, redfish, sheepshead, and gafftop. Nearby marinas and beachside shacks sell tackle and bait. For deep-sea fishing, you can hire a service to provide charter boats to take you out farther for big-time catches including snapper, marlin, king mackerel, and sailfish. Two reputable outfits are **Easy Going Charters** (979/233-2947, www.easygulffishing.com), which can accommodate up to six people on its 35-foot-long boat, and **Johnston's Sportfishing** (979/233-8513).

A popular place to spend a weekend of fishing, camping, and lounging is **Quintana Beach County Park** (330 5th St., 979/233-1461 or 800/872-7578, www.brazoria-county.com), located on a picturesque barrier island near Freeport. The park's multilevel fishing pier is a favorite among anglers, and the day-use facilities include shaded pavilions, restrooms, showers, and the historic Coveney House, containing a museum and natural history display. The camping sites include full hookups, showers, and laundry facilities. From Freeport, take FM 1495 south nearly two miles to County Road 723, then head east three miles to the park entrance.

Accommodations

Here's a nice change of pace: The Brazosport area is overrun with local lodging options, with nary a garish hotel chain sign in sight. Independently owned hotels are the norm, and many travelers opt to rent a beach house or cabin for the weekend.

HOTELS

Those looking for a clean, comfy place to stay within walking distance of the beach should consider the **Cedar Sands Motel** (343 Beach Dr. in Surfside Beach, 979/233-1942, www.cedarsandsmotel.net, $75–150, depending on room size and season). One-bedroom options are available, but you may want to splurge for the kitchenettes, including pots and pans, a queen-size bed, and pull-out bed. All rooms have refrigerators, microwaves, and free wireless Internet access. More casual and representative of many of the sun-bleached, wind-worn, slightly shabby beach hotels is **Surfside Motel** (330 Coral Ct. in Surfside Beach, 979/233-4948, www.surfside-motel.biz, $65–120). The motel offers kitchenettes with two queen-size beds, one twin bed, and a full kitchen, or two-room suites with one queen-size bed, a pull-out bed, small refrigerator, and microwave. Check with the front desk if you need beach towels, board games, or horseshoes.

Of course, chain hotels provide reliable consistency for some travelers; so, if slightly shabby isn't your thing, you'll have to venture four miles off the coast to the nearby community of Clute. The best option is **La Quinta** (1126 Hwy. 332 W., 979/265-7461, www.lq.com, $69 d), featuring free wireless Internet access, a free continental breakfast, and an outdoor pool. Another fine choice is **Holiday Inn Express** (1117 Hwy. 332 W., 979/266-8746, www.hiex-press.com, $107 d), offering wireless Internet access, a workout facility, and a free continental breakfast.

BEACH HOME RENTALS

Hundreds of rooms are available in cabins and

beach homes along the gulf in the Brazosport area. The best way to find something that fits your specific needs (pets, kids, weekends, beach access, etc.) is to contact a rental locating service. Two of the more commendable outlets in the area are **Beach Resort Services** (800/382-9283, www.beachresortservices.com) and **Brannan Resort Rentals, Inc.** (979/233-1812, www. brri.com). For a comprehensive list of companies, visit the following visitor-related sites: www. visitbrazosport.com and www.surfsidetx.org.

CAMPING

Families and RVers make repeated returns to **Quintana Beach County Park** (979/233-1461, www.brazoriacountyparks.com, $15–27), featuring 56 paved and level camping sites, full hookups, primitive tent sites, a bathhouse with restrooms, showers, and laundry facilities. Cabins—complete with TVs, microwaves, kitchenettes, and charming wooden detailing—are also available for rent, ranging from $135 to $160, depending on the season.

A popular option for anglers is **Surfside Beach RV Park** (102 Fort Velesco Dr., 979/233-6919, www.surfsidebeachrv.com, $25–30), offering full hookup RV sites, free parking for fishing boats, an on-site laundry, and free wireless Internet access.

Food

Let's assume you'll be spending most of your time at the beach. And we can presume you'll also be hungry at some point. The good news is, Surfside Beach has several good vacation-style eateries. The best of the bunch is the **Red Snapper Inn** (402 Bluewater Hwy., 979/239-3226, www.redsnapperinn.com, $9–21). This quality surf-and-turf restaurant is best known for its seafood items, including the grilled boneless flounder stuffed with crabmeat dressing, the fried soft-shell crabs with rémoulade sauce, bacon-wrapped oysters, and sautéed garlic shrimp. Turf-wise, most diners opt for the spaghetti and charbroiled Greek-style meatballs or the classic chicken-fried steak.

You can't miss **Kitty's Purple Cow** (323 Ocean Ave., 979/233-9161, www.kittyspurplecow.com, $4–9). The food isn't quite as attention-grabbing as the restaurant's facade, a distractingly purple building on the beach; regardless, Kitty's specializes in tasty meaty burgers and even a little seafood (boiled shrimp) from the unfortunately named "app-moo-tizers" menu. Breakfast is also available (after 10 A.M. on weekdays), with hearty portions of biscuits and gravy and standard egg dishes.

Locals loiter at the low-key **Jetty Shack** (412 Parkview St., 979/233-5300, $5–11), a beachside dive offering a tasty Angus burger, plenty of fried food, grilled cheese, and cold beer.

Any beach town worth its weight in sand dollars has a classic burger joint—in Surfside, it's **Castaway Bar & Grill** (979/233-7270, www.castawaybar.net, $5–12), where you can order a big ol' greasy burger and fries in-house or take out to complement the tasty waves.

Information and Services

The **Brazosport Visitors and Convention Council** (main office at 300 Abner Jackson Pkwy. in Lake Jackson, 979/285-2501 or 888/477-2505, www.brazosport.org) provides details on area attractions, accommodations, and restaurants, and brochures and maps to help you find your way around.

THE GULF COAST

Corpus Christi and Vicinity

Corpus Christi (population 285,267) is the largest city on Texas's Gulf Coast, and it's one of the most popular destinations in the state for seaside recreation, including fishing, sailing, swimming, and windsurfing.

The city has experienced a precipitous history, with drought, conflicts with Native American tribes, and various wars preventing settlements from taking hold until the mid-1800s, when a trading post was established and a small village developed that eventually became known as Corpus Christi, which translates as "the Body of Christ." Just when the town started growing, a yellow fever epidemic decimated the population, and it was subsequently plagued for decades by the lack of a deepwater port.

In 1916 and 1919, torrential storms destroyed portions of the city, erasing grand hotels and palatial homes. As a result, Corpus Christi, dubbed the "Sparkling City by the Bay," can appear historically lackluster, with a deficiency of significant structures reflecting its heritage. Regardless, historic homes and churches still exist in downtown neighborhoods unaffected by hurricanes and wrecking balls.

By the middle of the 20th century, Corpus, as it's known throughout the state, became a major petroleum and shipping center, with coastal shipments of gasoline, crude petroleum, and natural gas bringing increased corporate activity. Also contributing to the economy were the military bases and the petroleum and petrochemical industry, particularly the six refineries making good use of the approximately 1,500 oil wells in the area.

Despite its fairly large population, Corpus retains the feel of a small city, albeit one with remarkable museums and top-notch seafood restaurants. Corpus Christi's mild year-round temperatures and inviting tropical climate draw visitors from across the country to its cultural and recreational opportunities and abundant sunshine glistening on this "Sparkling City by the Bay."

SIGHTS
◖ Texas State Aquarium

The magnificent Texas State Aquarium (2710 N. Shoreline Blvd., 361/881-1200, www.texasstateaquarium.org, daily 9 A.M.–5 P.M., $15.95 adults, $14.95 seniors, $10.95 children ages 3–12, parking $4) offers an ideal way to take a quick break from the beach while still being surrounded by the region's fascinating natural resources. The layout of the aquarium is rather clever, leading visitors into Texas's marine world at sea level with exhibits containing birds, alligators, and stingrays, and proceeding to explore the Gulf of Mexico at sequentially deeper levels. One of the aquarium's main exhibits showcases menacing sharks, a 350-pound grouper, and hundreds of other species as they slither and glide around the barnacle-encrusted poles of a replicated offshore oil rig. The 350,000-gallon Dolphin Bay habitat uses seawater from Corpus Christi Bay for the Atlantic bottlenose dolphins that cannot live in the wild. A shaded seating area provides respite from the relentless sun for daily interpretive programs, and a lengthy viewing window allows visitors to get nose to nose with the dolphins. Other popular exhibits include Otter Space, featuring the frisky fellas cavorting on slides and in pools, and Living Shores, allowing kids to handle nonthreatening sea creatures. The aquarium expanded to include terrestrial critters, particularly in the Amazon rain forest exhibit, containing boa constrictors and poison dart frogs, and in the bird theater, featuring "flight performances" by hawks, falcons, and parrots. In 2010, the aquarium introduced Swamp Tales, an exhibit dedicated to conservation efforts in the region, especially with American alligators like Bo, the museum's featured 10-foot 'gator.

◖ USS *Lexington* Museum

You can't miss the massive USS *Lexington* Museum (2914 N. Shoreline Blvd., 361/888-4873, www.usslexington.com, open 9 A.M.–5 P.M.

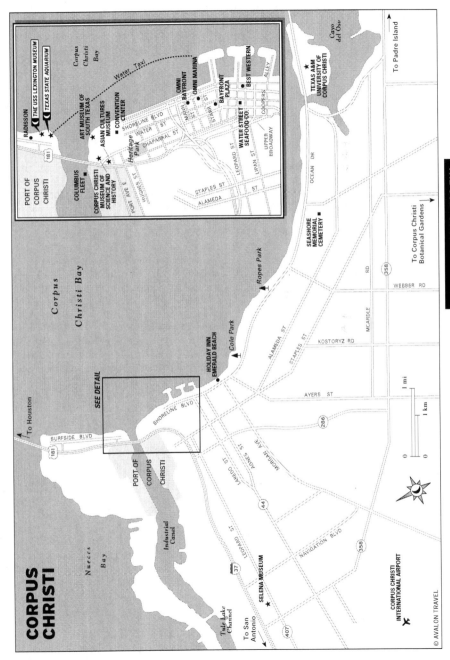

THE GULF COAST

CORPUS CHRISTI

Detail inset (top):

- PORT OF CORPUS CHRISTI
- RADISSON
- THE USS LEXINGTON MUSEUM
- TEXAS STATE AQUARIUM
- *Corpus Christi Bay*
- Water Taxi
- ART MUSEUM OF SOUTH TEXAS
- ASIAN CULTURES MUSEUM
- CONVENTION CENTER
- COLUMBUS FLEET
- CORPUS CHRISTI MUSEUM OF SCIENCE AND HISTORY
- SHORELINE BLVD
- *Heritage Park*
- WATER ST
- CHAPARRAL ST
- HUGHES ST
- PORT AVE E
- STAPLES ST
- ALAMEDA
- MANN ST
- OMNI BAYFRONT
- OMNI MARINA
- STARR ST
- BAYFRONT PLAZA
- WATER STREET SEAFOOD CO.
- BEST WESTERN
- PEOPLES ST
- LEOPARD ST
- LIPAN ST
- UPPER BROADWAY
- COOPERS ALLEY
- TEXAS A&M UNIVERSITY OF CORPUS CHRISTI
- OCEAN DR
- *Cayo del Oso*
- To Padre Island

Main map:

- *Nueces Bay*
- To Houston
- 181
- SURFSIDE BLVD
- *Tule Lake Channel*
- To San Antonio
- 407
- 37
- SELENA MUSEUM
- *Industrial Canal*
- PORT OF CORPUS CHRISTI
- LEOPARD ST
- LAREDO ST
- AGNES ST
- MORGAN AVE
- 44
- NAVIGATION BLVD
- 358
- CORPUS CHRISTI INTERNATIONAL AIRPORT
- SHORELINE BLVD
- SEE DETAIL
- *Corpus Christi Bay*
- HOLIDAY INN EMERALD BEACH
- *Cole Park*
- *Ropes Park*
- ALAMEDA ST
- STAPLES ST
- AYERS ST
- 286
- KOSTORYZ RD
- MCARDLE
- WEBBER RD
- 358
- OCEAN DR
- SEASHORE MEMORIAL CEMETERY
- To Corpus Christi Botanical Gardens
- 1 mi
- 1 km
- 0

© AVALON TRAVEL

the USS *Lexington*

daily Labor Day–Memorial Day, until 6 P.M. in the summer, $12.95 adults, $10.95 seniors/military, $7.95 children ages 4–12). Looming large in the Corpus Christi Bay, the USS *Lexington* is a decommissioned World War II naval aircraft carrier now serving as a 33,000-ton floating museum transporting visitors back in time with tours of the ship's decks and quarters, educational exhibits, restored aircraft, a high-tech flight simulator, and a collection of historical memorabilia. The music and voices blaring from speakers and interaction with the ship's docents gives an authentic feel for life aboard the nation's longest-serving aircraft carrier. The best way to experience the *Lexington* is via one of the five self-guided tours covering 100,000 square feet on 11 decks. Afterward, take some time atop the flight deck to soak up the view of the bay, the city skyline, and the impressive vintage aircraft.

Corpus Christi Museum of Science and History

To get a better sense of the area's colorful past, drop by the Corpus Christi Museum of Science and History (1900 N. Chaparral St., 361/826-4667, www.ccmuseum.com, Tues.–Sat. 10 A.M.–5 P.M., Sun. noon–5 P.M., $12.50 adults, $10 seniors, $6 children ages 5–12). The museum features myriad educational exhibits emphasizing the Gulf Coast's relation to the natural and cultural world. Particularly fascinating is the Ships of Christopher Columbus exhibit, featuring authentic reproductions of the *Niña, Pinta,* and *Santa Maria.* The three vessels, located outside the museum and accessible to visitors, were built in Spain to commemorate the 500th anniversary of Christopher Columbus's voyage to the New World. Each ship was made with authentic 15th-century materials such as hand-forged nails and wood from the same forests used for Columbus's ships. The museum's other noteworthy exhibits are also maritime related, including an interactive shipwreck display containing artifacts from three Spanish treasure ships that ran aground on Padre Island in 1554, an exhibit featuring artifacts related to French explorer Robert Cavelier, Sieur de La Salle's ill-fated *Belle* shipwreck, and the Children's Wharf, a bustling learning area for youngsters. The remainder of the museum contains a comprehensive collection of more than 28,000 objects (shells, Native American crafts, bird and reptile eggs) representing the history and culture of South Texas.

Heritage Park

Just down the street from the science museum is the city's Heritage Park (1581 N. Chaparral St., 361/826-3410, www.cctexas.com, Mon.–Thurs. 9 A.M.–5 P.M., Fri. 9 A.M.–2 P.M., Sat. 11 A.M.–2 P.M., guided tours Mon., Thurs., Fri. at 10:30 A.M., $6 adults, $2 children 12 and under). These 12 restored Victorian-era historic homes were moved to the city's cultural area to protect them from being demolished and to showcase the city's diverse past. The centerpiece is the Cultural Center's Galván House, open for free tours.

Asian Cultures Museum

Also located in the city's cultural district is the

Asian Cultures Museum (1809 N. Chaparral St., 361/882-2641, www.asianculturesmuseum.org, Tues.–Sat. 10 A.M.–4 P.M., $6 adults, $4 students, $3 children 12 and under), offering an interesting array of objects and artwork from across the Pacific. What started as a local resident's personal collection of cultural objects has evolved into a full-fledged museum containing thousands of items representing nearly a dozen Asian countries. Billie Trimble Chandler spent decades as a teacher and art collector in Asia, and brought items back to share with Corpus residents and educate them about faraway lands. Since then, the museum has grown to include clothing, furniture, paintings, dolls, statues, and other art objects from Japan, Korea, China, the Philippines, Taiwan, and other Asian countries. The museum also features international traveling exhibits and offers educational classes for students and the general public.

Selena Museum

Latin-music fans often make a pilgrimage to the Selena Museum (5410 Leopard St., 361/289-9013, www.q-productions.com, Mon.–Fri. 10 A.M.–4 P.M., $2 admission 12 and up, $1 children). It's not an easy place to find, however. The museum is located downtown just off I-37 in a warehouse-type building with no sign (look for the painted mural of Selena on the outside) and was created by Corpus resident Abraham Quintanilla to honor the memory of his daughter, the famous Tejana singer who was killed by the president of her fan club in 1995. The museum showcases many of Selena's personal memorabilia, including the outfits and dresses she designed and wore at concerts, her red Porsche, penciled sketches, her prized egg collection, and letters of sympathy from fans across the world.

Art Museum of South Texas

Culture converges at the Art Museum of South Texas (1902 N. Shoreline Blvd., 361/825-3500, www.stia.org, Tues.–Sat. 10 A.M.–5 P.M., Sun.

THE GULF COAST

LA SALLE'S LEGACY

French explorer Robert Cavelier, Sieur de La Salle left an enormous legacy in Texas. Though he's well known for his exploration in the Great Lakes region, La Salle's ambitious nature and tremendous hubris ultimately led to his demise after a doomed colonization effort on the Texas Gulf Coast.

In 1684, La Salle embarked on a mission to build forts along the mouth of the Mississippi River to attack and occupy Spanish territory in Mexico. His expedition proved to be a series of failures, beginning when one of his ships was captured by pirates in the West Indies and continuing with sickness, misdirection, and shipwrecks.

While searching for the mouth of the Mississippi, La Salle missed his target (by a wide margin – nearly 500 miles) and instead landed at present-day Matagorda Bay in the central Gulf Coast of Texas. One of his ships was lost offshore, and another, *La Belle*, became stranded on a sandbar during a storm.

La Salle made several more attempts to find the Mississippi, but they ultimately proved unsuccessful. Though he eventually established Fort St. Louis near the coast, his subsequent attempt to lead a party in search of reinforcements proved to be the last adventure this famed explorer would take – he was killed by his own men near present-day Navasota, Texas.

La Salle's legacy would be rekindled nearly 300 years later when his wrecked ship *La Belle* was discovered by marine archaeologists with the Texas Historical Commission. Considered one of the most important shipwrecks ever discovered in North America, the excavation produced an amazing array of finds, including the hull of the ship, three bronze cannons, thousands of glass beads, and even a crew member's skeleton. The artifacts have been carefully cleaned and preserved, and are currently displayed at numerous Gulf Coast museums.

1–5 P.M., $6 adults, $4 seniors and military, $2 students 12 and older). The three-story building is unmistakable, with bright white concrete walls and 13 rooftop pyramids overlooking the bay. Inside, you'll find several galleries showcasing the museum's 1,300 works of art, primarily paintings and sculpture representing the Americas with a focus on Texas, Mexico, and the Southwest. The museum also contains an interactive kids' playroom, classrooms, studios, a gift shop, and an auditorium.

Corpus Christi Botanical Gardens and Nature Center

Those who want to appreciate the area's natural beauty beyond the beach should visit the botanical gardens (8545 S. Staples St., 361/852-2100, www.stxbot.org, daily 7:30 A.M.–5:30 P.M., $6 adults, $5 seniors and military, $3 children ages 5–12). Exotic gardens and perfectly landscaped lawns await visitors at this popular attraction, which takes full advantage of its tropical climate to produce vibrant colors and lush landscapes. One of the center's showpieces is the Rose Garden, featuring 300 roses, a large pavilion, and beautiful lightly lapping fountain. Other noteworthy areas are the hummingbird garden, orchid garden with 2,500 flowering plants, and the hibiscus garden.

RECREATION
Beaches
CITY BEACHES ON THE BAY

If you're staying downtown and need a quick beach fix, go to **Corpus Christi Beach** (just north of the USS *Lexington*, 361/880-3480). It's not quite picturesque, and the shoreline sand is pretty coarse, but it's great for a leisurely stroll or swim with a pleasant view of Corpus Christi Bay. You'll see lots of local families playing in the sand or flying kites, and there are several spots offering rinse-off showers, restrooms, and small cabana huts with picnic tables. Much smaller in size yet within walking distance of downtown hotels is **Magee Beach** (Shoreline Blvd., at Park St., 361/880-3461). This 250-yard stretch of sand on the bay isn't designed for shell collecting, but it's a

good place to get your feet wet without worrying about them being pulled away by the undertow you'll encounter on the larger ocean beaches. Showers and restrooms are located on the north end of the beach.

ISLAND BEACHES ON THE GULF

Serious beachcombers and bodysurfers skip the bayside beaches and head straight to the long stretches of sand on the barrier islands 10 miles east of town on the Gulf of Mexico. Don't miss the beautiful shoreline along **Mustang Island State Park** (17047 State Hwy. 361, 361/749-5246, www.tpwd.state.tx.us, $4 daily ages 13 and older). Named for the wild horses that escaped from Spanish explorers and roamed free across this 18-mile long island, Mustang Island park comprises five miles of the pristine outstretched beach, perfect for swimming, fishing, sunbathing, hiking, biking, and even low-intensity surfing. Birding is another popular activity along this 4,000-acre island, notable for its distinctive ecosystem based on 20-foot-high sand dunes that protect the bay and mainland, and can reduce powerful hurricane-driven waves. To get there from Corpus, take South Padre Island Drive (Highway 358) to Padre Island, then head north on Highway 361 for five miles to the park headquarters.

Padre Island National Seashore

Just south of Mustang Island is Padre Island National Seashore (3829 Park Rd. 22, 361/949-8068, www.nps.gov/pais, $5 entry fee for walkers and bikers, $10 fee for vehicles, passes valid for seven days). Don't let the name fool you. This low-key, nature-oriented, protected shoreline is not to be confused with the commercial-minded party atmosphere of South Padre Island, a nearly three-hour drive to the south. Padre Island National Seashore is the longest remaining undeveloped stretch of barrier island in the world and appeals primarily to naturalists who delight in its primitive shoreline and birding and fishing opportunities. Birdwatchers arrive in droves during the fall and spring migration seasons when thousands of birds drop by the island, including sandhill

SAVE THE SEA TURTLES

Padre Island National Seashore is undertaking extensive efforts to protect an endearing creature that nests along its shoreline and glides among its gentle waves. The Kemp's ridley is the most endangered species of sea turtle, and it was nearly lost forever in the 1960s when a massive exploitation of eggs and meat occurred at its primary nesting beach in Mexico. The 16-mile stretch of sand at nearby Playa de Rancho Nuevo, Tamaulipas, Mexico, was home to nearly 40,000 Kemp's ridleys in 1947. Fewer than 5,000 currently nest each year.

Named for Richard M. Kemp, a fisherman who submitted the first documented specimen in 1906, the Kemp's ridley has been making a slow resurgence thanks to the devoted scientists with the National Park Service, which operates the Padre Island National Seashore between Corpus Christi and South Padre.

To help save the turtle, the U.S. and Mexican governments have been working together to reestablish a nesting beach at Padre Island National Seashore, utilizing the theory that turtles will return to the beach where they were born to lay their own eggs. For 10 years (1978-88), scientists collected more than 22,000 eggs at Rancho Nuevo and transported them in Padre Island sand to a lab at the national seashore for incubation. The hatchlings were released on the beach, where they then crawled to the surf with the hopes they'd be naturally imprinted with the location in their memories for future reference.

Park officials still incubate turtle eggs and release the little guys into the gulf each summer. The public is invited to view this fascinating natural event – for release dates and directions to the site, call the Hatchling Hotline at 361/949-7163.

Biologists have attempted to gauge the turtles' successful rate of return by marking their shells and fins with identification tags and even GPS devices. Their efforts appear to be productive, since each year more turtles revisit their birthplace. In fact, nearly 60 percent of the species' eggs are now found on Padre Island, making it the most important Kemp's ridley nesting beach in the United States.

Visitors who see a live or dead turtle on the beach are encouraged to immediately contact a park ranger or the seashore's turtle biologist at 361/949-8173. Messing with these endangered turtles in any way is considered a felony, with fines ranging up to $20,000. Many Kemp's ridleys have been identified and protected as a result of visitors' efforts, so perhaps your next stroll on the beach will yield a finding far more valuable than an intact sand dollar.

THE GULF COAST

cranes, hawks, and songbirds. The park is also considered the most important nesting beach in the country for the most endangered sea turtle in the world (Kemp's ridley). Park officials incubate sea turtle eggs found along the coast and release the hatchlings into the gulf during the summer. The public is invited to view this fascinating natural event—for release dates and directions to the site, call the Hatchling Hotline at 361/949-7163. Other popular activities at the park include swimming, fishing, windsurfing, and beachcombing. Visit the website for detailed information about camping locations and fees. To reach the park from Corpus, take South Padre Island Drive (Highway 358) to Padre Island, then head south on Park Road 22 for 13 miles to the Malaquite Visitor Center.

Fishing

Corpus is a major destination for anglers, and there are plenty of locations and services to accommodate them. You'll find anglers with poles anchored in the sand at several city beaches, including Corpus Christi Beach, where fishers often gather at the Nueces Bay Pier at the end of Hull Street. Lines are also cast along the bay on the massive concrete downtown piers (known locally as T-heads), several spots along the seawall, and at lighted breakwater jetties. Another popular spot is Bob Hall Pier at Padre Balli Park on North Padre Island. Its prime location and abundance of fish species (tarpon, mackerel, redfish, and even shark) have drawn anglers to this venerable and productive location since the 1950s. Bait and tackle are available at a nearby shop.

If you'd rather get out to sea for some big-game fishing, contact a charter or rental company to set you up with all the gear, guides, and good advice you'd ever want. Deep-sea boats are available for those who want to troll for Gulf of Mexico species such as marlin, sailfish, tuna, and kingfish. Reputable companies include **C&T Bay Charters** (4034 Barnes St., 888/227-9172, www.ctbaycharters.com) and Port Aransas–based **Deep Sea Headquarters** (416 W. Cotter Ave., 361/749-5597, www.deepseaheadquarters.com), providing private excursions to anglers of all ages and skill levels.

Windsurfing

Thanks to its constant easy breeze (averaging 15–20 mph), Corpus is a mecca for windsurfers. Although some try their sails on the bay at city locales like **Cole Park** (near the 2000 block of Ocean Dr., restrooms available), most windsurfers head to North Padre Island, particularly Bird Island Basin at the Padre Island National Seashore. This half-mile stretch of beach is internationally recognized as one of the top windsurfing sites on the U.S. mainland. If you've never grabbed hold of a sail, this is the best place to learn since there's always a breeze a blowin'. To set yourself up with all the gear, contact **Worldwinds Windsurfing** (11493 S. Padre Island Dr., 361/949-7472, www.worldwinds.net) or **Wind & Wave Water Sports** (10721 S. Padre Island Dr., 361/937-9283, www.windandwave.net).

Horseback Riding

Have you ever wanted to ride a horse on the beach, with the waves gently crashing at your trusty steed's feet as the ocean breeze whips through your hair? Then gallop over to **Horses on the Beach** (16562 S. Padre Island Dr., 361/443-4487, www.horsesonthebeachcorpus.com, several rides offered daily, reservations required), located just north of Padre Island National Seashore. Horses are available for first-timers, children, and experienced riders, and the stable owners also handle lessons. You're welcome to walk, trot, or ride your horse into the surf.

ENTERTAINMENT
Bars and Clubs

Though many visitors choose to sip their cocktails on the beach or in the hotel bar, there are options available for the adventurous souls who want to see some live music or perhaps even mingle with the locals. The best place to soak up the local scene without feeling like an outsider is the downtown **Executive Surf Club** (309 N. Water St., 361/884-2364, www.executivesurfclub.com). Located adjacent to the Water Street Seafood Co., the Surf Club's decor reflects its name, with vintage surfboards on the walls and refurbished as tables. The scene is lively yet casual, with live music most nights (mainly Texas rock and blues acts, often with a cover charge), more than 30 beers on tap, and a kitchen serving up tasty grub. Another visitor-friendly spot is the decidedly more upscale **Republic of Texas Bar & Grill** (900 N. Shoreline Blvd., 361/886-3515, www.omnihotels.com/republic). Sitting atop the 20th floor of the Omni Bayfront hotel, the Republic of Texas bar is dimly lit and heavily wooded in a welcoming way. The views of the bay and city are outstanding, the drinks are expertly made, and the pianist provides a perfect soundtrack. Grab a Scotch, margarita, or a draft beer and soak up the surrounding scenery.

Veering in a local direction is the younger and more boisterous **Dr. Rockit's Blues Bar** (709 N. Chaparral St., 361/884-7634, www.dr.ldescher.com). Located along a formerly vibrant stretch of Chaparral Street in the heart of downtown, Dr. Rockit's is still thriving, and it's still all about the blues. Live bands from Corpus and across the state play here nightly, and the place can get pretty rockin' when the bands get rollin'. Check the website for a live music schedule and cover charges. Just down the street is another laid-back locale, **Bourbon Street Bar and Grill** (313 N.

Chaparral St., 361/882-2082), a New Orleans–style establishment with Cajun food and free-flowing drinks. The activity kicks up a notch in Bourbon Street's Voodoo Lounge and next door at **Porky's Saloon.**

SHOPPING

Corpus has several malls that don't differ much from others across the country, and many of the vacationers looking for trinkets and T-shirts opt for the souvenir shops in Port Aransas. However, there are several places in town worth checking out that offer quality clothing and jewelry, imported goods, and beach gear. Among them is **Pilar Gallery** (3814 S. Alameda, 361/853-7171), a colorful shop with quality women's clothing, tapestries, rugs, and imported jewelry and folk art from Mexico and across the globe. You'll also find an amazing array of imports and curios at **El Zocalo Imports** (601 N. Water St. in the Omni Bayfront hotel, 361/887-8847). Though the primary focus here is Mexican jewelry, shoppers will find an interesting mix of objects, from crosses and candleholders to books and belt buckles.

Every beach city needs a good surf shop, and Corpus has several rad options to choose from. Hodads to heroes will find boards, surf wear, kayaks, skateboards, and surf and skate accessories at **Wind & Wave Water Sports** (10721 S. Padre Island Dr., 361/937-9283, www.windandwave.net) or **Worldwinds Windsurfing** (11493 S. Padre Island Dr., 361/949-7472, www.worldwinds.net).

ACCOMMODATIONS

There's no shortage of lodging options in Corpus, and most have decent views with easy access to the bay and fairly reasonable rates for a vacation destination. For those interested, there are plenty of budget options available in the airport/greyhound race track area, but most leisure travelers feel it's worth dropping the extra cash to stay in a place by the sea. If you're looking for a nice spot away from the city, consider a condo (nightly rates available) on alluring Mustang Island or North Padre

Island, about 10–15 miles from downtown directly on the Gulf Coast.

$50-100

You can do the beach on a bargain, if you consider lodging in the $90s a good deal. Not surprisingly, the more affordable hotels tend to be farther down the shoreline, but for many visitors, the key word is *shoreline,* so proximity isn't a concern. One of the better deals in town is the **Budget Inn & Suites** (801 S. Shoreline Blvd., 888/493-2950, www.budgetinnandsuitecc.com, $65 d), located within walking distance of Cole Park, one of the city's premier windsurfing spots. The hotel's amenities include a free continental breakfast, free wireless Internet service, and an outdoor pool and sundeck. A bit closer to the action is **Knights Inn** (3615 Timon Blvd., 361/883-4411, www.knightsinn.com, $94 d), located just a couple blocks off the bay and offering private balconies, several ocean-view rooms, free wireless Internet access, refrigerators, microwaves, and an outdoor pool.

Closer to downtown is the **Plaza Inn** (2021 N. Padre Island Dr., 361/289-8200, www.plazainnhotels.com, $99 d), offering a nice range of complimentary eats, from hot breakfast in the morning to popcorn and soda in the afternoon, and beverages and appetizers in the evenings. The Plaza Inn also has an outdoor pool, free Wi-Fi service, and is pet friendly. The best deal in the $100 range is **Quality Inn & Suites** (3202 Surfside Blvd., 361/883-7456, www.qualityinn.com, $99 d), thanks to its prime location on Corpus Christi Beach in the shadow of the USS *Lexington* and Texas State Aquarium. The hotel also features an outdoor beachside pool and hot tub, free continental breakfast, and rooms with microwaves and refrigerators.

$100-150

A reasonable deal in the heart of downtown is the **Bayfront Plaza Hotel** (601 N. Water St., 361/882-8100, www.bayfrontplazahotelcc.com, $109 d). The 10-story atrium lobby and interior corridor is pleasant, unless you're trying to get to sleep while a jazz band is enthusiastically playing in the bar. You can walk to restaurants and nightclubs from here, and even stroll down to the T-head piers or tiny Magee Beach. The hotel's amenities include a free breakfast, a large outdoor swimming pool, wireless Internet access, and free covered parking. A bit farther up the road in location and price is **Days Inn** (4302 Surfside Blvd., 361/882-3297, www.daysinn.com, $119 d), a block off Corpus Christi Beach. Amenities include rooms with microwaves, fridges, and free Wi-Fi access, along with a complimentary continental breakfast and outdoor pool.

A bit farther away from the bay is **Staybridge Suites** (5201 Oakhurst Dr., 361/857-7766, www.staybridgecc.com, $118 d). Features include a "sundowner reception" (Tuesday –Thursday) with complimentary light meals along with beer, wine, and soft drinks, as well as a free hot breakfast. Other amenities include a fitness center, whirlpool, outdoor pool, and free Wi-Fi service. Next door is the **Holiday Inn Express** (5213 Oakhurst Dr., 361/857-7772, www.hiexpress.com, $118 d), offering free Wi-Fi service, a complimentary hot breakfast bar, and a fitness center with an indoor pool and whirlpool.

A bit farther east is **Hilton Garden Inn** (6717 S. Padre Island Dr., 361/991-8200, www.hiltongardeninn.hilton.com, $119 d), offering a heated outdoor pool with Jacuzzi, complimentary high-speed Internet access, a microwave and minifridge in each room, and 32-inch flat-screen LCD TVs. Just off the busy South Padre Island Drive is **Hampton Inn** (5209 Blanche Moore Dr., 361/985-8395, www.hamptoninn.com, $119 d), which features free Internet access, a complimentary breakfast, to-go breakfast bags (on weekdays), an outdoor pool, and a fitness center.

Another downtown option is the **Best Western Marina Grand Hotel** (300 N. Shoreline Blvd., 361/883-5111, www.bestwestern.com, $139 d), offering rooms with private balconies and marina views, wireless Internet access, microwaves, refrigerators, a free continental breakfast, and an outdoor pool and

exercise facility. Farther south along the bayside is **Holiday Inn Emerald Beach** (1102 S. Shoreline Blvd., 800/465-4329, www.ichotelsgroup.com, $143 d). Also located along a nice stretch of beach, the Holiday Inn contains an indoor pool and fitness center along with an indoor recreation area for the kids (heated pool, Ping-Pong tables, billiard tables, vending machines, etc.). The hotel offers wireless Internet access and free meals for children.

The best choice for those who want to stay directly on the beach is the **Radisson** (3200 Surfside Blvd., 361/883-9700, www.radisson.com, $149 d). Step out the back doors and onto the sand of Corpus Christi Beach, a pleasant stretch of shoreline on the bay that hosts a large number of frolicking families, flotsam and jetsam, and the USS *Lexington*. Though the interior corridors are somewhat dark, the rooms are bright and cheery, with private balconies, microwaves, refrigerators, and free Internet access. The hotel features a splendid outdoor pool with swim-up bar service, a full-fledged fitness center, and a decent restaurant, the Blue Bay Grill.

$150-200

For something more intimate and less corporate, consider the new yet cozy **V Boutique and Hotel** (701 N. Water St., 361/883-9200, www.vhotelcc.com, $189 d). Located among the bayside businesses, the V features modern decor with a residential feel, including flat-screen TVs, free Internet access, fancy bedding, minibars, and a fitness center.

Looming large along the Corpus Christi Bay are the **Omni** towers, the Marina and Bayfront (707 and 900 N. Shoreline Blvd., 361/887-1600, www.omnihotels.com, $159 d). Located within a block of each other, the towers are connected by a walkway to form a deluxe complex. They're similar in price and amenities, although the Bayfront Tower offers additional upscale room options. Both towers provide rooms with wireless Internet access, free meals for kids, a fancy fully equipped health club, an indoor/outdoor heated swimming pool, an in-house massage therapist, bike rentals, and free covered parking.

Camping

An ideal spot for RVers looking to set up shop in town is **Puerto Del Sol RV Park** (5100 Timon Blvd., 361/882-5373, $25–35 nightly rates), located at the northern edge of Corpus Christi Beach. Amenities include full hookups, a rec room, laundry facilities, restrooms with hot showers, Internet access, and a book exchange. Farther out of town at the entrance of Padre Island is **Colonia Del Rey** (1717 Waldron Rd., 361/937-2435 or 800/580-2435, $25–35 nightly rates), offering a heated pool, hot tub, a recreation facility, laundry room, convenience store, and wireless Internet service. Nearby is the minimal yet affordable **Padre Balli Park** (15820 Park Rd. 22, 361/949-8121, $10–18 nightly rates), containing 54 paved campsites with water and electric hookups, 12 hardtop campsites for pitching a tent with water and electric hookups, and primitive camping on the beach. A bathhouse and laundry facility are also available.

FOOD

Seafood is the favored item on the menu for most Corpus Christi diners, and the variety of restaurants in the downtown area offers plenty of options. Since the city has such a large Hispanic population, you'll also find high-quality (and quantity) Tex-Mex restaurants.

American

By nature, beach towns are populated with casual eateries catering to flip-flopped families and sun-soaked seamen. Still, vacations are often an opportune time to celebrate the special occasion of being away from home in an exciting unfamiliar locale. A fancy meal is one of the best ways to commemorate a well-deserved break, and in Corpus, it doesn't get much fancier than the **Republic of Texas Bar & Grill** (900 N. Shoreline Blvd., 361/886-3515, $10–42). Located on the 20th floor of the Omni Bayfront hotel, this restaurant serves upscale Texas fare in a refined environment with incredibly stunning views. Meat is the main event here, and the range of options and methods of preparation are as impressive as the

surrounding scenery. Can't-miss menu items include Chateau steak with sautéed asparagus and broccoli, pork rib chops in an apple-ginger glaze, Texas crab cake with lobster and cognac sauce, and perfectly prepared venison, buffalo, and redfish.

One of the newer entries to the Corpus upscale food club is **Katz 21 Steak & Spirits** (317 N. Mesquite St., 361/884-1221, www. katz21.com, $13–39, closed Sun.). A traditional steak house specializing in prime grade-A beef, Katz's features quality cuts of beef as well as fresh seafood, veal, and lamb. Unlike many traditional stuffy steak houses, however, Katz's offers a lighter lunch menu with soups, salads, sandwiches, and pastas. Popular menu items include the prime rib served au jus with horseradish sauce, the bone-in rib eye, the rack of lamb, and veal picatta. Reservations are encouraged.

Slightly more trendy is **Dragonfly** (14701 Park Rd. 22 S., 361/949-2224, $8–23), offering a fresh take on seafood and other standard fare. The salmon has a wonderful curry seasoning and is accompanied by a tasty side of baby bok choy and carrots, while the cheesy lasagna somehow manages to be hearty without being overly filling. Other menu highlights include the slightly spicy shrimp skewer and tasty grilled tuna. Parents take note: Dragonfly doesn't officially have a kids menu, but they'll whip up a bowl of creamy mac and cheese upon request.

Okay, enough with the fancy stuff. Two of Corpus Christi's most venerable downtown eateries specialize in comfort food in a casual atmosphere. The 1950s-style **City Diner & Oyster Bar** (622 N. Water St., 361/883-1643, $6–16) is known for just about everything on the menu except its unremarkable oysters. From greasy burgers to zesty peppercorn ranch onion rings to classic chicken-fried steak to snapper smothered in a creamy crab and shrimp sauce, this retro establishment gets home-style regional fare right. Just a few blocks down the street is another esteemed local hot spot, the tourist-friendly **Executive Surf Club** (309 N. Water St., 361/884-7873, www.executivesurfclub.com, $7–16). This is an ideal place to grab a big ol' juicy cheeseburger and a Shiner Bock while you contemplate your next beach activity. Standard bar fare is the main draw here, and the Surf Club delivers with fish-and-chips, fried shrimp, tortilla wraps, and chicken-fried steak, all served on tables fashioned from old surfboards. Stick around after dinner for some local hot blues and rock bands.

Asian

Corpus has a long-standing connection with Asian cultures, reaching back nearly a century to the days when shrimpers and rice farmers arrived in the developing coastal town. Only recently, however, have Thai, Chinese, and Japanese restaurants come to the general public's awareness. Among the most popular is **Yalee's Asian Bistro** (5649 Saratoga Blvd., 361/993-9333, www.yaleesasianbistro.com, $6–18). The counter-service approach may lower expectations, but the food at Yalee's is top-notch, featuring popular menu items such as the spicy Ma Po tofu and flavorful standards like Kung Pao shrimp and General Tso chicken. Sushi fans should head directly to **Ichiban Japanese Seafood Buffet** (1933 S. Padre Island Dr., 361/854-6686, $7–19). There's something for everyone here, from classic tuna and shrimp rolls to more elaborate options such as octopus, unagi, hamachi, and squid. Since this is a buffet, diners also have the option of choosing oysters, crab legs, seaweed salad, and tasty barbecued short ribs.

Barbecue

Corpus isn't known as a barbecue mecca, but there are a couple noteworthy restaurants where out-of-staters can experience the mystique and magnificence of Texas-style 'cue. One of the better options is **Miller's Bar-B-Q** (6601 Weber Rd., 361/806-2244, $7–15). Miller's is known for its tender brisket and beef ribs, along with pork, chicken, and sausage. The sides here are better than average, so be sure to load up on the sweet potato salad and coleslaw.

Mexican

Unlike its seafood restaurants, most of Corpus Christi's Mexican spots are not on the waterfront. Regardless, several are worth the inland drive, particularly **La Playa** (5017 Saratoga Blvd. and 7118 S. Padre Island Dr., 361/986-0089, www.laplaya.cc, $7–18). This is the place to go for a top-notch traditional Tex-Mex meal. Feast on chicken enchiladas in a tangy tomatillo sauce or savor the sizzling beef fajitas. You won't regret ordering the stuffed fried avocados, either. This being a seaside town, you can also order Tex-Mex–style dishes featuring fresh fish and gulf shrimp. Another commendable spot offering some coastal flair to the Tex-Mex offerings is **La Costenita** (4217 Leopard St., 361/882-5340, $7–15, closed Sun.). This downtown eatery is small in size yet huge on taste, particularly the shrimp dishes and traditional enchilada and taco plates. Try not to fill up too quickly on the amazing chips and perfectly spicy homemade salsa.

Locals flock to **Kiko's** (5514 Everhart Rd., 361/991-1211, $6–15) for the enchiladas. Cheese enchiladas with zesty ranchero sauce are the specialty here, but you can't go wrong with most menu items, including the green chile burrito, guacamole salad, and tortilla soup. Better yet, sample all the goodness the restaurant has to offer with the Kiko's platter, offering a signature cheese enchilada, beef fajita tacos, and a crispy chalupa.

Also drawing Corpus crowds is **Solis Mexican Restaurant** (3122 Baldwin Blvd. and 5409 Leopard St., 361/882-5557, $6–14). This classic taqueria is known for its tasty tacos and enchiladas, all prepared with fresh homemade tortillas. Locals love their stuffed breakfast tacos (served all day) and *liquados* (fruity Mexican drinks).

Standard Tex-Mex is also the main draw at **Café Maya** (2319 Morgan Ave., 361/884-6522, $6–15), where you'll find massive plates of flavorful favorites such as beef enchiladas, chicken tacos, and cheesy quesadillas. For over-the-top goodness, order the shrimp-stuffed avocado.

Seafood

You'll catch the city's best seafood at **◆ Water**

Street Seafood Co. (309 N. Water St., 361/882-8683, www.waterstreetrestaurants.com, $8–19). In fact, if you're in Corpus for more than a day, it's practically required to eat a meal at this legendary downtown locale or at its adjacent sister location, Water Street Oyster Bar. Water Street takes everything tasty in the region—fresh seafood, Mexican influences, Cajun flavors, and good ol' Southern cooking—and combines it on the menu for the ultimate Texas Gulf Coast eating experience. For first-timers, the best place to start is the big blackboard, where you'll find fresh catches and daily specials (think blackened snapper, broiled flounder). The regular menu is equally appetizing, featuring consistently in-demand items such as crab cakes served with a spicy rémoulade and mango salsa; seafood jambalaya packed with shrimp, chicken, sausage, and crawfish tails in a creamy tomato sauce; and Southern-fried catfish stuffed with shrimp. Slightly more upscale and not quite as family oriented is the next-door **Water Street Oyster Bar** (309 N. Water St., 361/881-9448, www.waterstreetrestaurants.com, $8–22). This is a great spot to have a few cocktails and order some freshly shucked gulf oysters on the half shell. The menu is virtually the same as the Seafood Company's, so the aforementioned recommendations apply; you'll just be able to enjoy them in a more refined atmosphere. Two additional recommendations: Order your salad with the walnut-based tangy dressing, and try to save room for the hot chocolate brownie with ice cream.

One of the fanciest places in town to delight in a dish of succulent seafood while gazing upon its place of origin is the **Yardarm Restaurant** (4310 Ocean Dr., 361/855-8157, $10–30, Tues.–Sat. 5:30–10 P.M. only). This modestly sized, cozy spot (snug, even) offers tantalizingly fresh seafood, including succulent oysters, flavorful shrimp, a snappy snapper papillote, and thick, juicy steaks. Due to its limited size and popularity, reservations are recommended. On the opposite end of the sophistication scale is the consistently tasty yet way casual **Snoopy's Pier** (13313 S. Padre Island Dr., 361/949-8815, www.snoopyspier.com, $6–19). Located on the bay, Snoopy's is an ideal place to grab a cold beer and a plate full of fried or boiled shrimp. Watch the sun set as you lazily peel shrimp or enjoy the flaky goodness of fresh catches such as flounder or mahimahi.

If you're staying on Corpus Christi Beach, you'll find two quality laid-back seafood restaurants within walking distance of your hotel and the beach. **Pier 99** (2822 N. Shoreline Blvd., 361/887-0764, $7–21) is a Corpus Christi stalwart on the beach across from the massive USS *Lexington*. The portions here are nearly as big, particularly the combo plates overflowing with shrimp, crab legs, oysters, crawfish, and catfish. Be sure to order a bowl of the fresh seafood gumbo. Mellow live music keeps the atmosphere spirited most nights, providing a perfect Margaritaville moment for your tropical getaway. Not quite as aesthetically pleasing yet reliable in its good food is the misleadingly named **Blackbeard's On the Beach** (3117 E. Surfside Blvd., 361/884-1030, www.blackbeardsrestaurant.net, $6–19), located across the street from the Radisson and a couple blocks away from the ocean. This is another casual, family-friendly place where you'll find a bar full of bric-a-brac and hearty helpings of fresh seafood and Tex-Mex specialties.

INFORMATION AND SERVICES

The **Corpus Christi Area Convention & Visitors Bureau** (101 N. Shoreline Blvd., 361/881-1800 or 800/766-2322, www.visitcorpuschristitx.org) contains scores of brochures, maps, and helpful information on local attractions and recreation. Similar information is available at the bureau's downtown Corpus Christi Tourist Information center (1823 N. Chaparral St., 800/766-2322).

GETTING THERE AND AROUND

Located five miles west of downtown, the **Corpus Christi International Airport** (1000 International Blvd., 361/289-0171, www.cctexas.com/airport) offers service from several major airlines (Southwest, Continental, and American Eagle), including service to Monterey, Mexico. The city's bus system, **Regional Transportation Authority** (1806 S. Alameda St., 361/883-2287, www.ccrta.org), provides citywide service. Check the website for updated fare and route information.

PORT ARANSAS

When people say they're going to Corpus Christi to hit the beach, they're often referring to adjacent Mustang Island. Located at the northern tip of Mustang Island is Port Aransas (or Port A, as it's known locally), a charming little beach town with services catering to everyone from beach bums to big spenders.

Port Aransas's (population 3,905) origins are traced to an English farmer who used the area as a sheep and cattle grazing station in the mid-1800s. Decades later, New Jersey entrepreneur Elihu Ropes attempted to organize a massive project to dredge a 30-foot shipping channel across Mustang Island to allow access to the deep waters of the gulf. He was ultimately unsuccessful in his quest, but his efforts resulted in the town briefly being named Ropesville in his honor.

By the mid-20th century, Port Aransas became synonymous with recreation, drawing tens of thousands of anglers, swimmers, boaters, and beachcombers to its magnificent open beaches and charming seaside village atmosphere. The town's population swelled from 824 residents in 1960 to several thousand by the end of the century. As many as 20,000 vacationers descend on Port Aransas during peak periods, packing the island's motels, cottages, beach houses, condos, resorts, seafood restaurants, tackle shops, and boutiques.

To get there from the mainland, you'll have to travel across the South Padre Island Drive causeway from Corpus on the southern edge of the island, or, if you have the time and interest, take the 24-hour ferry from nearby Aransas Pass. It's well worth the effort. Look for dolphins behind the ferry as they tumble over each other in the bay snatching up fish in the boat's wake.

Marine Science Institute

At the risk of learning something on your beach vacation, consider a visit to the Marine Science Institute (630 E. Cotter Ave., 361/749-6729, www.utmsi.utexas.edu, Mon.–Fri. 8 a.m.–5 p.m., free admission). The oldest marine research station on the Texas Gulf Coast, the institute is dedicated to sciences (ecology, biochemistry, physiology, etc.) relating to plants and animals of the sea. Its visitors center offers educational movies (Monday–Thursday at 3 p.m.) and self-guided tours of marine related research project exhibits, stunning photographs, and seven aquariums containing offshore artificial reefs, black mangrove marsh, and Spartina, often over an open seafloor.

San Jose Island

If you're seriously into beachcombing—we're talking shell collections, mounted driftwood, maybe even a metal detector—then San Jose Island is your paradise. This privately owned property across the bay from Port Aransas is the definition of pristine—it's almost as untouched as it was when Karankawa Indians occupied the place nearly a thousand years ago. In the 1830s, locals found the remains of a pirate camp on the island, and rumor has it pirate Jean Lafitte's Spanish dagger with a silver spike is still somewhere guarding his booty of silver and gold. These days, "Saint Joe" is safe for visitors, who can access it via a short boat ride to partake of its premier swimming, fishing, sunbathing, and treasure hunting on this beautiful unspoiled property. To arrange transport, drop by Port A's **Fisherman's Wharf** (900 N. Tarpon St., 361/749-5448, www.wharfcat.com, call for seasonal rates).

Fishing

Port Aransas is a fishing mecca. Some claim the area is overfished, but it's clear to see why so many anglers are angling to get here—easy access to the bay and deep-sea gulf fishing provide species aplenty throughout the year. Those looking to keep their feet on solid ground or wooden dock can take advantage of the free fishing from beaches, jetties, or one of the three lighted piers (Charlie's Harbor Pier, Ancel Brundrett Pier, and J.P. Luby Pier) extending into the Corpus Christi Ship Channel. You'll have to pony up a dollar to use the popular and well-lit Horace Caldwell Pier, offering access to the gulf via Magee Beach Park. The pier is more than 1,200 feet long and open 24 hours day, with bait, tackle, rental equipment, and munchies available at a nearby concession stand.

Many anglers prefer the challenge of the larger deep-sea species, including kingfish, mackerel, red snapper, tuna, shark, and even mahimahi. Group boats offer bay and deep-sea fishing, and popular fishing tournaments take place throughout the summer. The Deep Sea Roundup, held each July, is the oldest fishing tournament on the Gulf Coast. As a testament to the overwhelming allure of fishing in Port A, the town has several hundred fishing guides. Inquire about group fishing at **Fisherman's Wharf** (900 N. Tarpon St., 361/749-5448, www.wharfcat.com), or to arrange a private rental, contact **Woody's Sports Center** (136 W. Cotter Ave., 361/749-5252, www.woodysonline.com).

Swimming

The best swimming in the area is at Mustang Island State Park, but visitors can still access portions of the wide and welcoming beach among the condos and private property just off the island's main road (Highway 361). Visitors can also swim and camp at the northern tip of the island just outside Port A at **Magee Beach Park** (321 North on the Beach, 361/749-6117, www.nuecesbeachparks.com). This 167-acre park isn't quite as breathtaking as other portions of Mustang Island or San Jose Island, but it's a good spot to dip your toes in the water and soak up the salty sea air. A park office offers limited visitor information, and the beach bathhouse contains publicly accessible showers.

Accommodations

INNS

For a truly memorable experience in this quaint seaside village, stay at the charming █ **Tarpon**

Inn (200 E. Cotter Ave., 361/749-5555, www.thetarponinn.com, $89–195, depending on room size and season). An "inn" in every sense of the term, this historic establishment offers a slice of life in the late 1800s. In fact, it's so authentic, you won't even find a TV (or phone!) in your room. Fortunately, Wi-Fi service is available, so if you prefer, you can get online and avoid doing old-fashioned things like book reading, relaxing in a rocking chair, playing croquet and horseshoes, or even talking. The rooms are small, but the lack of stuff in them—vintage beds and furniture notwithstanding—is imminently refreshing. Be sure to check out the old tarpon fish scales on the wall in the lobby, including those autographed by famous actors and politicians. The trolley stops out front every day to take guests to the beach or nearby shops.

Not quite as charming yet just as appealing in its localness is **Alister Square Inn** (122 S. Alister St., 361/749-3000, www.portaransas-texas.com, $89–189). Though it's a bit rough around the edges, this welcoming accommodation appeals to families and anglers alike with its various lodging options (two-bedroom apartments, kitchenette suites, and standard hotel rooms), each featuring microwaves, refrigerators, and wireless Internet access. Alister Square is within walking distance of the beach, shopping boutiques, and restaurants.

HOTELS

In Port Aransas, visitors have to pay more for the comfort of a familiar chain hotel than a local inn. Among the corporate options are **Best Western Ocean Villa** (400 E. Ave. G, 361/749-3010, www.bestwestern.com, $179 d), located within walking distance of beaches, fishing piers, and local shops. Amenities include rooms with microwaves, refrigerators, and Internet access, along with a free continental breakfast and an outdoor swimming pool. Closer to the beach (just a couple blocks away) is the **Holiday Inn Express** (727 S. 11th St., 361/749-5222, www.ichotelsgroup.com, $225 d), offering a fitness center, a pool and spa area, a free continental breakfast, and rooms with microwaves, refrigerators, and Internet access.

CONDOS

Condos proliferate Mustang Island's shoreline like barnacles on a shrimp boat. Albeit really nice barnacles. Condos make perfect sense in a beach environment—visitors can traipse back and forth between the surf and their temporary home, sand gathers guiltlessly on all surfaces, and beers and pizza fill the fridge. Perhaps most popular among the dozen or so options is **Beachgate CondoSuites & Motel** (2000 On The Beach Dr., 361/749-5900, www.beachgate.com, $230–310, depending on room size and season). Situated adjacent to the sandy shores of Mustang Island—meaning boardwalks or long trails through the dunes aren't necessary—Beachgate offers everything from efficiency-size motel rooms to full-size three-bedroom condos, accommodating everyone from the solo fisherman to the sizable family reunion. Larger options contain fully equipped kitchens, and all units have small refrigerators, microwaves, and coffeemakers. Additional amenities include a fish-cleaning facility, boat parking, and washers and horseshoe sets for fun on the beach.

Another commendable option is the **Sand Castle Condominium** (800 Sandcastle Dr., 361/749-6201, www.sandcastlecondo.com, $125–295), offering 180 units (efficiencies, one, two, or three bedrooms) with complete kitchens and laundry and maid service. The Sand Castle also features a fitness center, large outdoor pool and hot tub, a boardwalk to the beach, and a fish-cleaning facility.

Also drawing hordes of regulars is **La Mirage** (5973 Hwy. 361, 361/749-6030, www.lamirage-portaransas.com, $110–350), with clean and comfortable units in a three-story building surrounding a tropical courtyard. Options include studio efficiencies; one-, two-, or three-bedroom condos, each offering fully equipped kitchens; free Internet access; a laundry room; and living and dining areas.

Food

ITALIAN

There are two kinds of Italian restaurants in many coastal communities: beach grub and upscale cuisine. Port A has both. For a quick slice of pizza in an ultra laid-back environment, check out the immensely popular **Port A Pizzeria** (407 E. Ave. G., 361/749-5226, www.portapizzeria.com, $5–15, daily 10 A.M.–2 P.M., 5–9 P.M.). The biggest draw is the buffet, allowing diners to immediately devour hot slices of cheesy goodness. Some diners even choose to wait a few minutes for the tasty calzone. The big crowds usually ensure a quick turnaround on the pizza varieties.

The fancy Italian option in town is the consistently top-notch **Venetian Hot Plate** (232 Beach Ave., 361/749-7617, www.venetian-hotplate.com, $8–31, Tues.–Sat. 5–10 P.M.). Named for the sizzling iron plates some of the meals arrive on, this upscale spot specializes in tender and succulent meats, including filet mignon medallions, veal, and lamb. The wine selection is excellent, and the desserts are spectacular. Reservations are recommended.

SEAFOOD

One of the best seafood restaurants on the Gulf Coast is the unassuming yet spectacular ◖ **Shells Pasta & Seafood** (522 E. Ave. G, 361/749-7621, www.eatatshells.com, $9–31, Wed.–Mon. 11:30 A.M.–2 P.M., 5–9 P.M.). Housed inside a modest blue building, Shells is a tiny place—nine tables with plastic chairs—with an enormous reputation for quality fresh seafood and pasta dishes. Order from the daily blackboard specials or the regular menu, featuring classic and perfectly prepared seafood dishes such as the signature pan-seared amberjack, grilled shrimp, blue crab cakes, or sumptuous shrimp linguine in a delightfully creamy Alfredo sauce. This is elegant food in a casual shorts-wearing environment. Finding Shells will be a highlight of your trip to Port A.

Not quite as fancy yet well worth a visit is **Lisabella's** (224 E. Cotter Ave., 361/749-4222, $7–20, Mon.–Sat. 5:30–10 P.M.). Locals love Lisabella's mermaid soup, a tasty concoction of lobster, shrimp, coconut milk, curry, and avocado. The crab cakes and sautéed grouper are similarly enticing.

If you're looking for an ultracasual spot where you can wear T-shirts and flip-flops while gazing upon old fishermen's nets, mounted marlin, and the ocean itself, head to **Trout Street Bar & Grill** (104 W. Cotter Ave., 361/749-7800, www.tsbag.com, $8–24). Sit outside on the covered veranda to gaze upon the marina and ship channel activity while feasting on jumbo fried shrimp, grilled amberjack, snapper, tuna, or steak. A bonus: Trout Street will cook your fresh-caught fish as long as it's cleaned and ready for the kitchen.

Another venerable seafood spot is the "downtown" **Pelican's Landing Restaurant** (337 N. Alister St., 361/749-6405, www.pelicanslanding.com, $7–26). The portions are enormous here, and shrimp is the specialty. Go for the gusto and order one of the Mambo Combos (fried shrimp, steak, crab cakes, beer-battered fries) and savor the flavor on your surfboard table.

Information and Services

Pick up a handy brochure with island visitor info and a map of the trolley route at the **Port Aransas Chamber of Commerce and Tourist Bureau** (403 W. Cotter St., 361/749-5919, www.portaransas.org). The **Island Trolley** (aka "The B" and "The #94 Shuttle") will take you pretty much anywhere you want to go in Port A, from the beach to the wharf to shops and back to your hotel. For only 25 cents. It's particularly handy when you're on beer number four and dinner is calling. For more information about the trolley, contact the city at 361/749-4111.

The **Port Aransas Ferry System** provides free marine transportation service year-round at all hours of the day. The 15-minute ride connects Port Aransas with the mainland at Aransas Pass, north of Corpus Christi. There are six ferries in operation, each carrying up to 20 vehicles per trip. During the busy season, particularly holidays and some summer weekends, you may have to wait up to 30 or 45 minutes for a transport, but typically the wait is no longer than 5–10 minutes. For more information, call 361/749-2850.

KINGSVILLE

Located about 40 miles southwest of Corpus Christi, Kingsville (population 24,394) is the birthplace of the American ranching industry. It's the main commercial center of the legendary King Ranch, which sprawls across 825,000 acres and boasts 60,000 head of cattle.

The community is named for the famous riverboat baron and rancher Richard King, who used his business profits to purchase the vast piece of property that would become the legendary ranch. Kingsville's roots as a city are traced to the St. Louis, Brownsville and Mexico Railway, which put the town on the map when its tracks were laid in the early 1900s. Most of Kingsville's early business activity, however, was related to the King family, who started a weekly newspaper and built a hotel, an ice plant, and a cotton gin. Kingsville went on to become a busy trade center for ranching families across South Texas.

Kingsville's population grew significantly when Exxon relocated a district office here in the 1960s. A surge in enrollment at the Texas College of Arts and Industries (now Texas A&M Kingsville) brought even more folks to town, numbering nearly 30,000 by the late '70s. Exxon closed its regional office in 1985, and the population has slowly declined since then.

Regardless, Kingsville remains a major draw for birders and naturalists, who delight in the area's million acres of habitat. Visitors from across the state and the country travel to the historic downtown area to learn about the heritage of King Ranch and to shop at the boutiques and antiques stores.

King Ranch

For many Texas visitors, King Ranch is the embodiment of the Lone Star State's legacy. Longhorn cattle, vast ranchlands, and genuine cowboys evoke a sense of mystique and grandeur that Texas alone can claim.

THE GULF COAST

As improbable as it may seem, America's ranching legacy was revolutionized by a man who arrived as a preteen stowaway on Texas's Gulf Coast. Richard King, who escaped from New York City in 1835 aboard a cargo ship, went on to become a steamboat baron along the Rio Grande before overseeing his ranching empire.

The origins of King Ranch, now an esteemed National Historic Landmark, date to 1853 when Richard King purchased 68,500 acres of property that had been Spanish and Mexican land grants. Between 1869 and 1884, King sent more than 100,000 head of livestock from his ranch to northern markets on now-legendary routes like the Chisholm Trail. Many of these herds were marked with the iconic symbol for the King Ranch, the Running W brand, which first appeared in the 1860s. Though the origins of this distinctive shape aren't known, local legends claim it represents the sweeping horns of a longhorn bull or a slithering diamondback rattlesnake.

One of King Ranch's biggest claims to fame is its development of the Western Hemisphere's first strain of beef cattle: Santa Gertrudis. Based on the name from the property's original land grant, this breed of cattle was developed in the 1920s to produce cows that could withstand the oppressive South Texas conditions—heat, humidity, and biting insects. To accomplish this, breeding experts (including Richard King's grandson) crossed Indian Brahman cattle with British Shorthorns.

King was also one of the first ranchers to move Texas Longhorns from Mexico to markets in the Midwest, and the innovations developed at his ranch, from cattle and horse breeding and disease control to improving the blood lines of the quarter horse to well drilling, earned it the proud title "birthplace of American ranching."

Today, King Ranch sprawls across 825,000 acres, an area larger than the state of Rhode Island. The **King Ranch Visitor Center** (2205 Hwy. 141 W., 361/592-8055, www. king-ranch.com, Mon.–Sat. 11 A.M.–4 P.M., Sun. noon–5 P.M., $8 adults, $4 children ages

5–12) offers daily guided tours along an old stagecoach road past majestic Longhorns with the iconic Running W brand on their hindquarters, and a 100-year-old carriage house with a mission-style roofline and distinctive arches. Other highlights include the Victorian-era cabin homes of King's working families (known as Kineños) and a horse cemetery with graves of famous racing thoroughbreds from the 1950s. Bring plenty of water, since it gets plenty hot out on the ranch. Special tours devoted to birding, native wildlife, and agriculture are available in advance by reservation.

To learn more about the fascinating history of the King family and property, move 'em up and head 'em a couple miles down the road to the **King Ranch Museum** (405 N. 6th St. in Kingsville, 361/595-1881, www.king-ranch. com, Mon.–Sat. 10 A.M.–4 P.M., Sun. 1–5 P.M., $4 adults, $2.50 children ages 5–12). Housed in a historic downtown ice plant, the museum contains stunning 1940s photos of the ranch by award-winning photographer Toni Frissell, fancy saddles and firearms, antique coaches and carriages, and other historic ranch items. One of the most intriguing objects on display is "El Kineño," a custom-designed 1949 Buick Eight hunting vehicle—complete with rifle holders and a shiny Running W hood ornament—made by General Motors especially for Congressman R. M. Kleberg Sr.

Another must-see (and smell) is the restored 1909 Ragland Mercantile Building that now houses the leather-filled **King Ranch Saddle Shop** (201 E. Kleberg Ave., 877/282-5777, www. krsaddleshop.com, Mon.–Sat. 10 A.M.–6 P.M.). Originally used to supply gear exclusively to the King Ranch cowboys known as *Los Kineños* (King's people), the store now offers leather goods and clothing to the world (its website does brisk business). The charming downtown shop also contains exhibits and photos on ranch history and information about the governors, presidents, and foreign dignitaries it has outfitted.

1904 Train Depot and Museum

Located a block away from the saddle shop is the restored 1904 Train Depot and

KING'S PEOPLE

© TEXAS HISTORICAL COMMISSION

the gates of the legendary King Ranch

At the heart of the King Ranch are the Kineños (King's people), a group of several hundred ranch employees whose families have dedicated their lives to operating the property for generations. From training horses to clearing fields to promoting the King Ranch's original cattle breed, the Kineños provide a vital link with the ranch's past and are responsible for maintaining its ongoing legacy.

If you schedule a visit to the ranch or take part in one of the tours, you'll likely get a chance to visit with one of these Kineños. Several now serve as visitor guides, even though they occasionally take on some of their traditional ranch-hand duties. By the way, many of these are men in their 80s.

Some of these men spent their early days "breaking" thoroughbred horses. In the 1940s and '50s, King Ranch trained racing horses and developed many well-known and successful thoroughbreds. The Kineños also worked extensively with the ranch's quarter horses, using the handling techniques passed down through generations of *vaqueros* (Mexican cowboys).

Other Kineños worked closely with the Santa Gertrudis cattle breed, specifically developed and marketed by the ranch. They helped promote the breed by attending livestock shows across the world and even slept in the barns with the animals and woke up early to clean, feed, water, and brush the cattle in preparation for the shows. Kineños also worked with the breed by administering vaccinations, helping in the pastures, and maintaining records.

Some of these stories have been captured for posterity's sake in print. For a fascinating collection of colorful Kineño tales, pick up a copy of Alberto "Beto" Maldonado's book *The Master Showmen of King Ranch* (University of Texas Press, 2009).

Kingsville's 1904 Train Depot and Museum

Museum (102 E. Kleberg Ave., 361/592-8515, www.1904-depot.kingsvilletexas.com, Mon.–Fri. 10 A.M.–4 P.M., Sat. 11 A.M.–2 P.M., free admission), offering a glimpse into Kingsville's bustling past. Photos and artifacts, including an operational telegraph, highlight the historical significance of this hub of regional activity.

Kenedy Ranch Museum of South Texas

Richard King isn't the only famous rancher in these parts. His longtime pal Mifflin Kenedy also accumulated great wealth and property thanks to his successful commercial and ranching endeavors. His legacy is on display at the Kenedy Ranch Museum of South Texas (200 E. La Parra Ave., 361/294-5751, www.kenedyranchmuseum.org, Tues.–Sat. 10 A.M.–4 P.M., Sun. noon–4 P.M., $3 adults, $2 seniors and children ages 13–18). Located 20 miles south of Kingsville in the little town of Sarita, the museum showcases Kenedy's illustrious past through exhibits

dedicated primarily to family, particularly his wife's, Petra Vela de Vidal, of prominent Mexican heritage. Through his successful business ventures, Kenedy accumulated 400,000 acres of Gulf Coast property and was among the first ranchers to hold cattle inside wire fences. Housed in the 1927 Kenedy Ranch headquarters, the museum also details the family's many successful philanthropic programs.

John E. Conner Museum

Regional history and the natural world are the main areas of interest at the John E. Conner Museum (905 W. Santa Gertrudis Ave., 361/593-2810, www.museum.tamuk.edu, Mon.–Fri. 9 A.M.–5 P.M., Sat. 10 A.M.–4 P.M., free admission). Located on the campus of Texas A&M-Kingsville, this modest museum offers exhibits devoted to the cultural groups that have historically occupied the area, from Native Americans to Spanish to Mexican and pioneer settlers. Native plant and animal species and their environments are also on display, as well as artwork from students and Texas artists.

Accommodations

If you find yourself making an overnight trip to Kingsville, there are only a few options available for lodging. Fortunately, one of them is the **Holiday Inn Express** (2400 S. Hwy. 77, 361/592-8333, www.hiexpress.com, $99 d), offering a free hot breakfast bar, Wi-Fi access, and a heated outdoor pool. If you want to experience "rustic" ranch lodging, check out the **B Bar B Ranch Inn** (325 E. County Rd. 2215, 361/296-3331, call for rate info), which sits on property that was originally part of the King Ranch. This B&B on a working ranch provides "rugged pampering," with its hearty gourmet breakfast and 16 guest rooms decorated in South Texas style. The B Bar B draws a good number of people who enjoy using the surrounding ranchland to hunt for antelope, turkey, and quail.

Food
AMERICAN

Kingsville isn't a highly regarded destination for fine dining, but there are a few places worth dropping by if you're visiting King Ranch or even headed down to South Padre. One of the best places to eat in the entire region is about 20 miles south of Kingsville in a tiny town called Riviera. ◖ **King's Inn** (1116 S. County Rd. 2270, 361/297-5265, $12–24, closed Sun. and Mon.) is billed as one of the best seafood restaurants on Texas's southern Gulf Coast, and for good reason. It doesn't look like much from the outside, and the outdated ambience isn't really charming either, but that matters not as soon as your food arrives. Be sure to order the lightly breaded fried shrimp, filled with freshly caught flavor and accompanied by the restaurant's famous spicy tartar sauce (the waiter claimed to be sworn to secrecy, though he eventually let it slip that the tartar sauce contained bread crumbs, "lots of eggs," and serrano peppers). This stunning sauce enhances everything from the interesting choice of fish (drum) to the homemade

bread to the avocado salad with accompanying slices of fresh, juicy tomatoes. It's absolutely worth the 20-minute detour to eat like a King.

Just south of the downtown area is an ideal lunch spot, the occasionally rowdy **Big House Burgers** (2209 S. Brahma Blvd., 361/592-0222, $5–10). The sports bar atmosphere can be a bit overwhelming on weekends (reminding you there's a college in this town), but it's worth enduring the noise and blaring TVs for the immense and flavorful burgers. Try the quadruple burger if you dare. These juicy treats will fill you up, but it's still worth splitting some of the crunchy fries or crispy onion rings with a pal.

MEXICAN

One of the most popular places in town to grab an authentic Tex-Mex meal is **El Tapatio Mexican Restaurant** (630 W. Santa Gertrudis St., 361/516-1655, $7–14), on the edge of Kingsville A&M campus. Though most of the food is standard Tex-Mex fare, there are a few items that set El Tapatio apart from other spots in town. The carne guisada, in particular, is spectacular, with a hearty gravy that brings out the rich flavor of the beef. Like the salsa, it has an extra kick and afterbite that leaves your mouth feeling warm and satisfied.

Another worthy local eatery is **Lydia's Homestyle Cooking** (817 W. King Ave., 361/592-9405, www.lydiasrestaurant.com, $6–16, Mon.–Sat. 5 A.M.–1:30 P.M.). Lydia's is known throughout town for its tremendous breakfast taquitos (try the potato, eggs, and sausage) and the machacado plate, featuring shredded dry beef scrambled with eggs along with grilled onions, tomato, and serrano peppers. Lydia's lunches are legendary, too, including the barbacoa plate, tamales, and chicken flautas. If necessary, you can also order gringo fare (burgers, sandwiches, etc.).

Another reputable Mexican restaurant is **El Dorado** (704 N. 14th St., 361/516-1459, $6–13). There's nothing too fancy here, but the traditional Tex-Mex fare is consistently decent, including the beef tacos, chicken enchiladas, and burritos.

Information and Services

For information about other area attractions, accommodations, and restaurants, visit the **Kingsville Convention and Visitors Bureau** (1501 Hwy. 77, 361/592-8516, www.kingsvilletexas.com, Mon.–Fri. 9 A.M.–5 P.M., Sat.–Sun. 10 A.M.–2 P.M.).

South Padre Island

The massive 130-mile-long Padre Island is home to the longest sand beach in the United States. Never stretching more than three miles wide, the island was formed by the methodical process of sea erosion and deposition. The northern portion, adjacent to Corpus Christi, has a modest collection of hotels and residences, and is mostly recreation oriented; the central portion is the natural protected wonderland of Padre Island National Seashore; and the southern tip is a major resort area lined with hotels and restaurants catering to a thriving tourist industry.

South Padre Island isn't technically a separate island; rather, it's the name of the resort community at the southern portion of the big island. The town is flanked by the Gulf of Mexico to the east, a narrow ship channel to the north, and the Laguna Madre, the narrow bay leading to the Texas mainland.

Spanish explorers visited the area in the 1500s, but the resort community remained a barren stretch of pristine seashore until the 1950s when a causeway bridge connected Port Isabel to South Padre Island. Although it provided access to the nicest beaches on the Texas coast, the community remained a low-key resort destination until the late 1970s when insurance companies were required to provide hurricane coverage and the population increased rather dramatically (from 314 to 1,012 residents) thanks to the increased emphasis on tourism. For the past two decades, it's become a major spring break destination for college students, who descend on the small town in the thousands for revelry and recreation each March.

SIGHTS

Island time is good for the soul. Everything slows down, priorities shift to beach activities and seafood options, and even the tightly wound lay off their car horns. It may take a day or two to assimilate to South Padre mode, but once you're there, you won't want to leave.

South Padre is the ultimate beach vacation in Texas. Its soft, smooth sand is far more inviting and picturesque than the grainier, darker versions farther north along the coast. The resort community offers everything seaside travelers seek—beachcombing, fishing, parasailing, dolphin viewing, biking, snorkeling, and scuba diving. Lodging options range from opulent resort condos to pitching a tent on the beach, and restaurants offer gulf-harvested oysters, shrimp, and fish.

If you're visiting in the winter, you'll be surrounded by Midwestern license plates and polite retirees taking advantage of restaurants' early-bird specials. In the summer, Texas families flock to the island to play in the gentle waves and devour fried shrimp. Any time of the year is a good time to visit South Padre, since the beach is always pleasant and the vibe is always mellow (except during spring break).

The islanders take their enviable natural resources seriously, offering opportunities for visitors to experience the wonders of this region. Make a point of taking a dolphin tour and visiting the sea turtle research center to get a true appreciation of the sea life that doesn't end up on your dinner plate.

Though it takes some effort to get to South Padre, once you're there, maneuvering around the small town is a breeze. After crossing the Queen Isabella Causeway, take a left onto Padre Boulevard to reach the main drag, with hotels, shops, and restaurants. Take a right off the causeway to reach the public beaches and seaside attractions.

Sea Turtle, Inc.

A heartwarming experience awaits at Sea Turtle, Inc. (6617 Padre Blvd., 956/761-4511, www. seaturtleinc.com, Tues.–Sun. 10 A.M.–4 P.M., $3 donation requested), an unassuming little spot at the end of South Padre's main strip. Inside, you'll find tanks full of various types and sizes of sea turtles, several native to the nearby Gulf Coast. Try to arrive at 10 A.M. for the informative presentation offering context about the several dozen friendly and fascinating creatures on-site. Kids can feed the turtles, and everyone has a chance for a photo op. Marvel at these prehistoric animals—some can reach 450 pounds—and toss an extra few dollars in the box for this organization that works tirelessly to protect and promote these endangered sea creatures.

Dolphin Research and Sea Life Nature Center

Kids aren't the only ones who'll learn something at the nearby Sea Life Nature Center (110 N. Garcia St. in Port Isabel, 956/299-1957, www. spinaturecenter.com, daily 10 A.M.–6 P.M., $3 donation requested). This low-key locale just across the causeway from South Padre contains about 20 aquariums filled with sea creatures from the gulf waters. Shrimp, starfish, rays, and eel await at the center, which offers a children's program at 11 A.M. and 2 P.M. allowing youngsters to handle and feed some of the nonthreatening species in the touch tanks. Knowledgeable staffers educate visitors about environmentally responsible ways to enjoy their time on the island.

◖ Port Isabel Lighthouse

It's well worth the 74-step climb up the tight spiral staircase to experience the breathtaking views from the Port Isabel Lighthouse (421 E. Queen Isabella Blvd. in Port Isabel, 800/527-6102, www.tpwd.state.tx.us, summer hours: Sun.–Thurs. 10 A.M.–6 P.M., Fri.–Sat. 11 A.M.–8 P.M., winter: daily 9 A.M.–5 P.M., $3 adults, $1 students). From the bug-size cars passing over the gorgeous Laguna Madre

a rescued sea turtle at South Padre's Sea Turtle, Inc.

© ANDY RHODES

THE GULF COAST

© ANDY RHODES

THE GULF COAST

the Port Isabel Lighthouse near South Padre

Bay on the San Isabella Causeway to the remarkable view of adjacent historic downtown Port Isbell, the vantage point from this historic lighthouse is truly a sight to behold. Constructed in 1852 at the request of sea captains frustrated by visibility issues along the low-lying Texas coast, the lighthouse was a prominent and necessary fixture in the region until the early 1900s, when newer, more efficient, and more powerful towers were constructed. Sixteen similar lighthouses graced the Texas coast at one time, but the Port Isabel structure is the only facility remaining open to the public.

Pan American Coastal Studies Laboratory

Not quite as family oriented as other area attractions, the coastal studies lab (100 Marine Lab Dr., 956/761-2644, www.utpa.edu/csl, Sun.–Fri. 1:30–4:30 P.M., free admission) is designed more with researchers in mind than kiddos. Regardless, you'll learn things here about the plant and animal life in the Laguna Madre and Gulf of Mexico through interactive displays (shark jaws, turtle shells) and limited aquariums.

Schlitterbahn Beach Waterpark

Despite the fact real waves are lapping at the shore just minutes away, families still flock to the water rides at Schlitterbahn Beach Waterpark (33261 State Park Rd. 100, 956/772-7873, www.schlitterbahn.com, open 10 A.M.–8 P.M. daily April–Sept., $40–48). Without any pesky sand and saltwater to worry about, kids and adults can spend the day gliding and cruising along water trails and rides, including popular attractions such as tube chutes, the Boogie Bahn surfing ride, uphill water coasters, and the Rio Ventura. Unlike the original Schlitterbahn in New Braunfels, which is far more spread out with more meandering, lazy inner tube rides, the South Padre version is more compact and beach oriented, with a five-story sand castle fun house and a surprisingly good restaurant (the Shrimp Haus).

RECREATION
Swimming

The beach is everywhere at South Padre, so you won't have any trouble finding a place to park and tote your gear to the soft, white sand (don't forget to bring plenty of sunscreen and bottled water). Look for public beach access points every few blocks along Gulf Boulevard. For a few more amenities—pavilions, picnic tables, and playgrounds in addition to the restrooms and showers—go to one of the county beach parks on the southern or northern ends of the island.

Fishing

Like most coastal communities, fishing is a huge draw in South Padre. Everywhere you look, you'll see men (and the very occasional woman) with a fishing pole standing on a beach, jetty, or pier. If they aren't standing on shore, they're in a chartered boat. Shoreline anglers tend to snag redfish, speckled trout, and flounder, while deep-sea adventurers seek

SPRING BREAK AT SOUTH PADRE

This low-key, unassuming beach community turns into a high-octane, raucous party town for several weeks each March. Nearly 100,000 students from across the country descend on South Padre Island from approximately March 10 through March 20, prompting locals to skedaddle from their quiet seaside homes quicker than a college kid can chug a beer.

Rivaling Florida's Daytona Beach as the nation's ultimate spring break destination, South Padre has become party central for college students primarily from Texas and the Midwest. Though the town doesn't quite have the infrastructure to handle the hordes – eight-hour waits on the causeway are common on peak arrival days – it ultimately benefits from the millions of dollars spent on lodging, food, and DWI tickets (be forewarned: take the Wave shuttle if you've had a few drinks).

Speaking of drinking, one of South Padre's biggest spring break assets is its on-the-beach consumption policy – unlike most American seashores, it's completely legal here if you're 21 or older. The undercover TABC (Texas Alcoholic Beverage Commission) agents are out in full force looking for MIPs (minors in possession), so make sure you're of legal age or at least extremely discreet. In other drinking-related news, visitors may want to consider renting a hotel with kitchenette or, even better, a condo for easy access to a fridge, ice, and countertops. For a comprehensive list of condo options, visit www.service24.com.

Spring breakers often take advantage of the various package deals offered by travel agencies. Most involve flights and lodging, but several feature miniexcursions around the area for those seeking a brief respite after four or five days of constant drinking and sunbathing. One of the most popular activities is a professionally operated surfing lesson, complete with board, wet suit, and individual instruction. Those in search of a change of scenery while downing drinks can sign up for a party yacht cruise originating at Tequila Frogs, one of South Padre's most famous bars.

tarpon, marlin, kingfish, mackerel, red snapper, and wahoo.

Many anglers use the services of the venerable **Jim's Pier** (209 W. Whiting St., 956/761-2865), which bills itself as the original South Padre Island fishing-guide company. Jim's provides boat slips, fueling docks, a launching ramp, and fish-cleaning facilities. The company also offers two bay fishing trips daily on its renowned 40-person-capacity party boat. To find out more about fishing locations and services, consult the **Port Isabel/South Padre Island Guides Association** at www.fishspi.com, offering a lengthy list of endorsed professional fishing guides.

Dolphin Viewing

Even though you don't technically get in the water to take on this activity, it's ocean based and certainly worth experiencing. The Laguna Madre Bay is home to myriad bottlenose dolphins, and

there's nothing like the thrill of seeing them up close in their natural environment. The best way to get an intimate experience is through an independent tour company like **Fins to Feathers** (tours operate from Port Isabel's Sea Life Center, 956/299-0629, www.fin2feather.com; tours run daily 7 A.M.–sunset and cost $22.50 or $45 per person depending on the amount of time desired). Enjoy the quiet, smooth ride from a smaller boat allowing up-close views and facilitated interaction with the knowledgeable guide. Anticipate the surge of excitement you'll feel when that first dorsal fin ascends from the water and the sun glistens off the smooth gray surface of these magnificent and elegant creatures.

Snorkeling and Scuba Diving

With its clear water and fine sand, the South Padre Island area is a haven for scuba divers and snorkelers. The fish aren't as varied and colorful as you'll find in more exotic tropical

© ANDY RHODES

dolphin tour in Laguna Madre Bay

locales, but the marine life is certainly intriguing, and you never know what you might find among the reefs and rigs.

Those interested in snorkeling and shallow shore dives can explore the underwater action at the Mansfield Jetties, the beach at Dolphin Cove (look for sand dollars here), and the adjacent Barracuda Bay. Scuba divers will enjoy the artificial reef (a wreck dive known as "the tug") located seven miles southeast of the Brazos Santiago Pass Jetties. Farther out and most compelling to experienced divers are the oil rigs, where fish of all sizes are plentiful.

South Padre has several full-service dive shops offering equipment for rent and sale, organized excursions to prime spots, instruction, and service. One of the most reputable companies is **American Diving** (One Padre Blvd., 956/761-2030, www.divesouthpadre.com).

ACCOMMODATIONS
Hotels and Resorts

Lodging rates in a beach town are akin to those in a ski village—they can be mile-high in the busy season and downright affordable the rest of the year. The following South Padre

accommodations include prices for a weekend stay in midsummer (the busy getaway season in Texas, despite the fact it's 93 degrees and humid).

Among the affordable options is **South Beach Inn** (120 E. Jupiter Ln., 956/761-2471, www.southbeachtexas.com, $49–149, depending on room size and season), an independently owned 12-unit establishment nestled among the palms just a block from the beach. One of the oldest hotel buildings on the island (1961), South Beach offers mostly efficiency-style kitchenettes with full-size stoves, refrigerators, microwaves, and toasters. Pets are welcome, and Wi-Fi service is available. Also in the affordable range is **Beachside Inn** (4500 Padre Blvd., 956/761-4919, www.padrebeachside.com, $99 d), featuring clean, simple rooms within walking distance of the beach, an outdoor pool with hot tub, and kitchenettes with microwaves and refrigerators.

The next step on the price ladder gets you a bit closer to the action with some added amenities. One of the more popular and reliable options is the **Ramada Limited** (4109 Padre Blvd., 956/761-4097, www.ramadasouthpadreisland.

com, $139 d), offering a free hot breakfast, an outdoor pool and hot tub, and rooms with microwaves, fridges, and free wireless Internet access. Closer to the Queen Isabella Causeway is the casual yet consistent **Super 8** (4205 Padre Blvd., 956/761-6300, www.super8.com, $153 d), offering a heated outdoor pool, free continental breakfast, free Wi-Fi access, and mini microwaves and refrigerators. Another trustworthy chain option is **Holiday Inn Express** (6502 Padre Blvd., 956/761-8844, www.hiexpress.com, $179 d). What sets it apart from the other corporate choices is the massive aquarium in the lobby with dozens of colorful fish darting about. Otherwise, the amenities here are pretty standard, including an outdoor pool, a fitness center, beach access, Wi-Fi access, and rooms with microwaves and refrigerators. The **Travelodge** (6200 Padre Blvd., 956/761-4744, www.southpadretravelodge.com, $184 d) offers a large outdoor pool and hot tub, a private walkway to the beach, free wireless Internet access, a deluxe continental breakfast, and microwave and refrigerators in each room.

Occupying 15 tropical beachside acres is **Sheraton South Padre Island Beach Hotel** (310 Padre Blvd., 956/761-6551, www.starwoodhotels.com, $179 d), a comfortable yet fancy spot with ample amenities and several types of accommodations. Choose from standard guest rooms, kitchenettes, suites, or even fully equipped two- and three-bedroom condominiums, all with private balconies. Other amenities include an enormous 6,000-square-foot swimming pool complete with waterfall and swim-up bar, a separate oversize Jacuzzi, volleyball nets, an exercise and weight room, and seasonal parasailing. Another option is **Best Western La Copa Inn & Suites** (350 Padre Blvd., 956/761-6000, $149 d), offering free Internet service, a free deluxe continental breakfast, and nightly happy hour with beer, wine, and snacks. Just down the street is the upscale **Peninsula Island Resort & Spa** (340 Padre Blvd., 956/761-2514, www.peninsulaislandresort.com, $280 d), featuring one-, two-, and three-bedroom units with kitchenettes, a swim-up pool bar, large edgeless pool, hot tub,

rooms with fancy Brazilian furniture, a gym, and an on-site convenience store.

Among the most luxurious choices on the island is the **Isla Grand** (500 Padre Blvd., 800/292-7704, www.islagrand.com, $279 d), boasting perhaps the best beachfront location in town with excellent services. Rooms include free Internet access, microwaves, and refrigerators. Consider upgrading to a condo suite—the spacious rooms, living area with a couch and second TV, fully equipped kitchen, and separate bathrooms (a godsend for those with kids) provide a perfect home away from home. It's the hotel's grounds, however, that keep guests coming back for repeated recreational relaxation. Enjoy the direct beach access, two outdoor swimming pools with a cascading waterfall, three whirlpools, four lighted tennis courts, shuffleboard courts, and plenty of lounge chairs.

Camping

Beachfront property is too valuable to allow for many camping options in the commercial area of South Padre. In fact, there's really only one main option for serious RV-style campers, and fortunately it's a swell one. The **South Padre Island KOA** (1 Padre Blvd., 800/562-9724, www.southpadrekoa.com, $30–60 nightly) is geared toward RVs and mobile homes, but it also has a few cabins and lodges available. Site amenities include an outdoor pool, a fitness center, recreation room, and free wireless Internet service. Those looking for a more rustic, natural experience have the option of pitching a tent (or parking an RV) on the vast unpopulated stretch of sand north of all the major recreational activity. Local officials caution campers to drive on the wet sand to avoid getting stuck in the soft tractionless powder farther away from the surf. Also, be sure to bring your garbage back with you (there aren't any trash cans in these remote areas) and take the No Trespassing signs seriously.

FOOD
Seafood

One of the first places many beach-town visitors go is a seaside seafood restaurant. Even before you check in to your hotel room you may want to drop by a low-key local eatery like **Palm Street Pier Bar & Grill** (204 W. Palm St., 956/772-7256, www.palmstreetpier.com, $7–18), known for its tantalizing seafood and sunsets. Overlooking the scenic Laguna Madre Bay, Palm Street Pier specializes in tasty shrimp dishes, including admiral shrimp (sautéed in a sweet potato–jalapeño puree), honey chipotle shrimp, and the standard crispy fried variety. Other popular dishes include the tilapia fillet and rib eye steak. Don't miss the cheap margaritas and summertime Friday-night fireworks over the bay. Another bonus: the "you hook it, we'll cook it" policy, allowing diners to bring in their own fresh catch and have it expertly prepared—blackened, grilled, or fried with two sides—for $6.

Also drawing regular return customers is the venerable and well-regarded **Blackbeard's** (103 E. Saturn Ln., 956/761-2962, www.blackbeardsspi.com, $7–20), a swashbuckling-themed spot with surprisingly refined food. Fresh gulf catches are the main draw here, including flounder and tilapia, but the landlubber options are equally commendable, including the charbroiled steaks and grilled chicken. Incidentally, the burgers here are the best on the island.

For the ultimate sampling of seafood, belly up to the buffet at (**Louie's Backyard** (2305 Laguna Dr., 956/761-6406, www.lbyspi.com, $9–26). Choose from boiled shrimp, crab legs, fish, and scallops along with ribs, pasta, and salad. The full menu has even better options, including a buttery and flaky red snapper fillet and crispy, flavorful fried shrimp. Top off your experience with a stunning view of the sunset over the bay while sipping Louie's signature cocktail, the multiliquored and aptly named Whammy.

South Padre also has a couple highly recommended seafood restaurants that are more upscale in nature. In a casual town like this, however, that simply means the quality and prices are higher—you can still wear shorts and sandals. One of the most popular is the remarkable (**Sea Ranch Restaurant** (1 Padre Blvd., 956/761-1314, www.searanchrestaurant.com, $9–40), the kind of place where you can't go wrong with anything on the menu, be it "from

the sea" or "from the grill." The options change regularly, but the mantra of the Sea Ranch remains constant: serving quality "local wild-caught" seafood directly from the gulf. Signature dishes include grilled red snapper, boiled king crab legs, gulf shrimp and bay oysters, and an amazing ahi tuna served rare with soy sauce and wasabi. Topping it all off is an exceptional view of the sea. Reservations are suggested.

Another popular semiupscale seafood spot is **Scampi's Restaurant & Bar** (206 W. Aires Dr., 956/761-1755, www.scampisspi.com, $8–39, open for dinner only), an old-school seafood and steak restaurant that's been around for decades thanks to its consistent high-quality food and service. Scampi's proves that venerable doesn't have to mean boring, with several innovative and unexpected dishes on the menu. The best of the bunch is the shrimp Marco Antonio, featuring sautéed shrimp with coconut milk, mango, apples, and a touch of habanero pepper. Locals love the peanut butter shrimp, an Asian-inspired recipe with ginger, garlic, soy sauce, and peanut butter. Other featured entrées include pecan redfish, crawfish penne, and local flounder, pompano, and amberjack.

Beach Grub

If you've somehow exhausted your craving for seafood, your next best bet is some standard beach fare—burgers, pizzas, fried stuff, and, in South Padre, Tex-Mex. One of the best places in town to combine all these things with a cold glass of quality suds is **Padre Island Brewing Company** (3400 Padre Blvd., 956/761-9585, www.pibrewingcompany.com, $6–17). Not surprisingly, beer is the main theme here, with home-brew supplies such as kettles, burlap sacks, and vintage bottles serving as surrounding scenery. It's a refreshing change of pace from the ubiquitous corporate light-beer signs in most beach establishments. Fortunately, the handcrafted beer is commendable, particularly the Tailing Red Amber. There's food, too, including traditional bar fare like burgers, nachos, ribs, and sandwiches. Look for a seat on the second-floor outdoor deck.

Slightly more upscale yet equally inviting

is **Amberjack's Bayside Bar & Grill** (209 W. Amberjack St., 956/761-6500, www.amberjacks-spi.com, $9–34), offering incredible views of Laguna Madre and a wide range of delectable menu items. Choose from oysters Rockefeller to chicken-fried chicken to rasta shrimp (prawns sautéed in curry sauce) to pecan-crusted chicken. Pull up directly to the restaurant in your boat and take advantage of Amberjack's "we'll cook your catch" policy.

For a tasty burger and cold beer, head to **Tom & Jerry's Beach Bar & Grill** (3212 Padre Blvd., 956/761-8999, $6–18). The seafood dishes here are commendable, but the beach grub is the main draw, from the burgers to the chicken plates to the chicken-fried steak and club sandwich. After your meal, head to the raised bar, where friendly staffers will gladly pour you a cold draft beer or expertly mix a frozen concoction.

Finally, if you're in the mood for some traditional Tex-Mex, head to the extremely popular and immensely satisfying **Jesse's Cantina & Restaurant** (2700 Padre Blvd., 956/761-4500, $7–15). Jesse's is famous for its potent margaritas and top-notch traditional dishes such as tacos, enchiladas, carnitas, and quesadillas. Naturally, they serve fried shrimp here, too, and it's some of the best on the island.

INFORMATION AND SERVICES

The incredibly friendly and helpful people at the **South Padre Island Convention & Visitors Bureau** (600 Padre Blvd., 800/767-2373, www.sopadre.com, Mon.–Fri. 8 A.M.–5 P.M., Sat.–Sun. 9 A.M.–5 P.M.) will provide you with brochures, maps, and information about area attractions. You can also check with them about activities and events related to fishing, boating, and other ocean-based recreation.

GETTING THERE AND AROUND

The Brownsville South Padre Island International Airport (700 S. Minnesota Ave., 956/542-4373, www.flybrownsville.com) is the closest airport to South Padre. At 27 miles away, it's not too far, especially if you need to get to the beach in a hurry and don't feel like making the nearly nine-hour drive from Dallas or approximately five-hour trek from Houston and Austin. The airport offers several American Eagle and Continental Airlines flights daily to and from Houston. Rental car services are available at the airport.

Once on the island, feel free to ditch the car in favor of the city's reliable and often-necessary **Wave transportation system** (866/761-1025, visit www.townspi.com for schedule and stops). If you plan to have a beer or six during spring break, you'll be glad these small buses are there to cart your impaired body safely home. Though the Wave typically operates 7 A.M.–7 P.M. among local businesses and services, it's also available during spring break to shuttle late-night revelers. Incidentally, the belligerent scene on the ride back from the bar at 3 A.M. is one of the most insane experiences imaginable.

THE GULF COAST

www.moon.com

DESTINATIONS | ACTIVITIES | BLOGS | MAPS | BOOKS

MOON.COM is ready to help plan your next trip! Filled with fresh trip ideas and strategies, author interviews, informative travel blogs, a detailed map library, and descriptions of all the Moon guidebooks, Moon.com is all you need to get out and explore the world—or even places in your own backyard. While at Moon.com, sign up for our monthly e-newsletter for updates on new releases, travel tips, and expert advice from our on-the-go Moon authors. As always, when you travel with Moon, expect an experience that is uncommon and truly unique.

MOON IS ON FACEBOOK—BECOME A FAN!
JOIN THE MOON PHOTO GROUP ON FLICKR

MAP SYMBOLS

▨▨▨	Expressway	(€	Highlight	✗	Airfield	⚲	Golf Course
▨▨▨	Primary Road	○	City/Town	✗	Airport	▣	Parking Area
▨▨▨	Secondary Road	◉	State Capital	▲	Mountain	▤	Archaeological Site
• • • •	Unpaved Road	⊛	National Capital	✦	Unique Natural Feature	▮	Church
- - - -	Trail	★	Point of Interest			▤	Gas Station
• • • • •	Ferry	•	Accommodation	✺	Waterfall	◌	Glacier
- - - -	Railroad	▼	Restaurant/Bar	▲	Park	▨	Mangrove
▨▨▨	Pedestrian Walkway	▪	Other Location	▯	Trailhead	▨	Reef
▥▥▥	Stairs	⋀	Campground	✗	Skiing Area	▱	Swamp

CONVERSION TABLES

°C = (°F − 32) / 1.8
°F = (°C x 1.8) + 32
1 inch = 2.54 centimeters (cm)
1 foot = 0.304 meters (m)
1 yard = 0.914 meters
1 mile = 1.6093 kilometers (km)
1 km = 0.6214 miles
1 fathom = 1.8288 m
1 chain = 20.1168 m
1 furlong = 201.168 m
1 acre = 0.4047 hectares
1 sq km = 100 hectares
1 sq mile = 2.59 square km
1 ounce = 28.35 grams
1 pound = 0.4536 kilograms
1 short ton = 0.90718 metric ton
1 short ton = 2,000 pounds
1 long ton = 1.016 metric tons
1 long ton = 2,240 pounds
1 metric ton = 1,000 kilograms
1 quart = 0.94635 liters
1 US gallon = 3.7854 liters
1 Imperial gallon = 4.5459 liters
1 nautical mile = 1.852 km

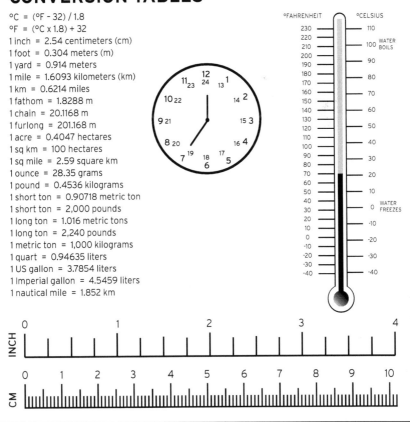

MOON SPOTLIGHT HOUSTON & THE TEXAS GULF COAST

Avalon Travel
a member of the Perseus Books Group
1700 Fourth Street
Berkeley, CA 94710, USA
www.moon.com

Editor: Shaharazade Husain
Series Manager: Kathryn Ettinger
Copy Editor: Justine Rathbun
Graphics Coordinator: Darren Alessi
Production Coordinator: Darren Alessi
Cover Designer: Kathryn Osgood
Map Editor: Kat Bennett
Cartographer: Kaitlin Jaffe, Kat Bennett

ISBN: 978-1-59880-967-1

Printed in the United States

ABOUT THE AUTHOR

Andy Rhodes

Andy Rhodes has been living and traveling in Texas since 1994. He calls Austin home, but regularly explores the Texas Hill Country, East Texas pine forests, and Gulf Coast beaches. His favorite destination is the Big Bend region of far West Texas, where the enormous sky and rugged mountains beckon with the promise of solace, serenity, and low humidity.

Since 2002, Andy has thoroughly covered the state as editor of the Texas Historical Commission's magazine The Medallion, offering him an opportunity to experience the Lone Star State's compelling heritage in both colossal cities and tiny towns. In the process, he's developed a keen appreciation for Texas's vernacular architecture and savory barbecue.

Andy's freelance articles have been published in *Home & Away, American Cowboy,* and *Austin Monthly* magazines, and his work has appeared in the *Austin American Statesman* newspaper. In 2009, Andy was named a featured author and served as a panelist at the prestigious Texas Book Festival.

Andy earned a journalism degree from Ohio's Miami University in 1993. He lives in Austin with his wife Paula and sons Max and Daniel.